Praise for *Transform Your Beliefs, Transform Your Life*

'Transform Your Beliefs, Transform Your Life *brings together the power of EFT with the epigenetic understanding that negative beliefs, formed and held subconsciously during early childhood, need to be addressed if a person is to heal from stress-related issues in their life.'*
BRUCE H. LIPTON PhD, BESTSELLING AUTHOR OF THE BIOLOGY OF BELIEF

'Energy psychology is nothing less than the medicine of the future. These deceptively simple processes have the power to help you overcome the most debilitating of emotions, from grief to depression. By wedding two disciplines, this book offers a comprehensive toolkit to help reprogramme your thoughts and reclaim your life.'
LYNNE MCTAGGART, INTERNATIONAL BESTSELLING AUTHOR OF THE FIELD, THE INTENTION EXPERIMENT AND THE BOND

'So often the beliefs that control our destiny are unconscious. Transform Your Beliefs, Transform Your Life *provides a tremendous resource for anyone who wants to learn how to gain new awareness, take their power back and live the life they choose! This book draws on the experiences of the thousands of people who have trained in this technique, and the information and expertise is rich and varied. It's a fantastic resource to come back to again and again.'*
JESSICA ORTNER, NEW YORK TIMES BESTSELLING AUTHOR OF THE TAPPING SOLUTION FOR WEIGHT LOSS AND BODY CONFIDENCE

'This book is a treasure trove of guidance for anyone wanting to heal themselves from their past. With this new book, Karl Dawson and Kate Marillat provide us with invaluable exercises, insights, techniques and wisdom from not only their own, but also their practitioners' years of experience and expertise. It deserves to be on the bedside table of anyone wanting to move forward in their lives with ease and grace.'
SONIA CHOQUETTE, NEW YORK TIMES BESTSELLING AUTHOR OF THE ANSWER IS SIMPLE

'It takes only one loving thought to undo an entire belief system based on fear. Let Karl and Kate show you how.'
ROBERT HOLDEN PhD, AUTHOR OF HAPPINESS NOW! AND SHIFT HAPPENS!

'This gem of book delivers what it promises. I love the clarity that shines light into the complexity of how beliefs can hold you back. Karl and Kate's straight-talking approach uses lots of great examples to make it easy for anyone to grasp the essence of the Matrix Reimprinting technique. It's also a great refresher and enhancer for those familiar with this work.'

ARIELLE ESSEX, AUTHOR OF PRACTICAL MIRACLES

'This brilliant book does exactly what it says in the title. Transform Your Beliefs, Transform Your Life explores the big benefits of finding and fixing your unhelpful beliefs, and provides readers with ample encouragement that 'you can do it too'. If you believe that your beliefs are standing in your way of realizing optimum health, wealth and happiness, then I highly recommend using the techniques shared within this transformational book.'

SANDY C. NEWBIGGING, BESTSELLING AUTHOR OF MIND CALM

'So many people fail to understand the power of their belief system and how it affects their lives. Reading this book will help anyone to examine their perceptions of the world – and more importantly, transform them. It's rare to find such advice and practical tools in such a simple format.'

DONNA GATES, BESTSELLING AUTHOR OF THE BODY ECOLOGY DIET

'During my work as a radio presenter I have interviewed hundreds of experts in the self-development field. Whilst interviewing Karl Dawson I found that EFT Matrix Reimprinting joined together many scientifically proven ideas I know to be true with a practical answer for personal transformation. I was so excited that I decided to bring EFT Matrix Reimprinting into my own work with clients, with jaw dropping results! Now, with Transform Your Beliefs, Transform Your Life, Karl and Kate have created an easy-to-understand, practical guide to transforming your life that anyone can pick up and start to reap the benefits from immediately. By reading this book you are joining a wave of personal transformation that is building momentum and has the potential to free humanity from the unconscious beliefs holding us back. I'm delighted you have found this book and I thank Kate and Karl for bringing it to life.'

BECKY WALSH, AUTHOR, PRESENTER, COMEDIAN AND LIFE-HACK CATALYST

Transform Your
BELIEFS,
Transform
YOUR LIFE

TRANSFORM YOUR
BELIEFS,
TRANSFORM
YOUR LIFE

EFT Tapping using
Matrix Reimprinting

KARL DAWSON WITH KATE MARILLAT

HAY HOUSE

Carlsbad, California • New York City • London • Sydney
Johannesburg • Vancouver • Hong Kong • New Delhi

First published and distributed in the United Kingdom by:
Hay House UK Ltd, Astley House, 33 Notting Hill Gate, London W11 3JQ
Tel: +44 (0)20 3675 2450; Fax: +44 (0)20 3675 2451; www.hayhouse.co.uk

Published and distributed in the United States of America by:
Hay House Inc., PO Box 5100, Carlsbad, CA 92018-5100
Tel: (1) 760 431 7695 or (800) 654 5126
Fax: (1) 760 431 6948 or (800) 650 5115; www.hayhouse.com

Published and distributed in Australia by:
Hay House Australia Ltd, 18/36 Ralph St, Alexandria NSW 2015
Tel: (61) 2 9669 4299; Fax: (61) 2 9669 4144; www.hayhouse.com.au

Published and distributed in the Republic of South Africa by:
Hay House SA (Pty) Ltd, PO Box 990, Witkoppen 2068
Tel/Fax: (27) 11 467 8904; www.hayhouse.co.za

Published and distributed in India by:
Hay House Publishers India, Muskaan Complex, Plot No.3, B-2,
Vasant Kunj, New Delhi 110 070
Tel: (91) 11 4176 1620; Fax: (91) 11 4176 1630; www.hayhouse.co.in

Distributed in Canada by:
Raincoast Books, 2440 Viking Way, Richmond, B.C. V6V 1N2
Tel: (1) 604 448 7100; Fax: (1) 604 270 7161; www.raincoast.com

A catalogue record for this book is available from the British Library.

ISBN: 978-1-78180-376-9

Interior images: 9 © Arielle Essex; 46, 72–73 © Karl Dawson & Kate Marillat; 78 © Silvia
Hartmann; 129, 137 © Within-Sight Training & Consultancy; 198 © Janice Thompson

Printed and bound in Great Britain by TJ International Ltd, Padstow, Cornwall

This book is dedicated to Matrix Reimprinting practitioners around the world. It is through your passion and commitment to this body of work that it has grown beyond our wildest dreams.

CONTENTS

FOREWORD

For several years, Karl and I were like ships in the night. We kept missing each other at conferences and events – even when we were going into the filming for the *Choice Point* movie; we passed each other by five minutes.

How apt that when we did finally meet we were both in the front row at a Hay House conference, listening intently to one of our heroes – Dr Bruce Lipton. After the talk I spent a lot of time chatting to Karl about Matrix Reimprinting and how Bruce Lipton's work underpinned so much he was passionate about; as a scientist, this therapy made complete sense to me.

Fast-forward a few years and I was presenting at the Matrix Reimprinting Convention and totally inspired by the audience's energy and enthusiasm for this technique. There were over 200 people in the room and the vibration was sky high. The community of people using this technique for their own wellbeing and happiness, and for the happiness of others, has reached large numbers in just a few short years.

What I (and I suspect the Matrix community) love about Matrix Reimprinting is that Karl has joined up the dots between the power of beliefs, the placebo effect, scientific evidence and how the mind and body store trauma. I've supported Karl's work from the early days, and as a scientist it makes me incredibly joyful to read the evidence and research paper included in this book from Professor Antony Stewart and Dr Elizabeth Boath, which further aids its efficacy.

Understanding our belief system is central to my work as both a scientist and an author. I've always been fascinated by the placebo effect – how people's health improves through believing they are receiving a drug. Karl and Kate have taken this understanding and laid it out in such a way that readers will understand how their belief systems are formed. Beliefs are fluid like water, they gain momentum and strength and are our lifeblood, yet if we are caught in a torrential rapid of a belief without a boat or a paddle, it can be our downfall. Essentially, beliefs touch everything in our lives, and at the centre of how we act and react to any situation is our belief system, what we learned from early childhood experiences, our parents and our culture.

But here's the good news – no matter what you believe, it's possible to transform those beliefs with Matrix Reimprinting, and as a result, transform your biology. To have a therapy that focuses on beliefs is ground-breaking. Doing self-work in the matrix and connecting with our past selves makes so much sense to me.

In this book, Karl and Kate give the reader everything they need to carefully navigate serious life areas such as pain management, depression and abuse with grace and clarity. It is full of empirical evidence that shows how deep this work goes, from spider phobias and a mother who had lost her child and was able to reconnect with him in the matrix, to the banker with a million-dollar bonus.

Matrix Reimprinting is simple to learn and intensely practical. It's underpinned with science and, put simply, if you want to believe positive things about yourself, then this book is for you. If you transform your belief system, you can transform your experience of reality.

DAVID R. HAMILTON PhD
AUTHOR OF HOW YOUR MIND CAN HEAL YOUR BODY

INTRODUCTION

Our thoughts are so fast it's hard to catch them. But why do we 'think' a particular thought or 'feel' a particular way in the first place?

New science is proving that it is our core beliefs that control our thought patterns, provide fuel for our emotions, drive the chemical changes in our body and essentially produce our reactions and attractions to the external world.

Karl Dawson knows first-hand that core beliefs underpin everything in a person's life, no matter what traumas they have experienced. Seven years since the birth of his revolutionary technique, Matrix Reimprinting, and thousands of case studies and hundreds of trainees later, he now ensures that practitioners focus on core beliefs to achieve true and sustainable change in both their own and their clients' lives.

Why Read This Book?

This book will introduce you to the Matrix Reimprinting technique so you can effectively transform any core belief into a positive force in your life. We will show you the basics of Matrix Reimprinting and how you can use this self-acceptance tool to its full potential. We also aim to give you an interactive textbook that examines important life areas in detail. We have consulted Matrix Reimprinting practitioners all over the world who work specifically in these areas, so we are able to present you with the latest information, techniques, resources, questions and adaptations to enhance your own work with Matrix Reimprinting.

The first Matrix Reimprinting book, *Matrix Reimprinting Using EFT* (Hay House, 2010), which Karl co-authored with Sasha Allenby, paved the way for the understanding that it is our beliefs that underpin all of our current behaviour and experiences. *Transform your Beliefs, Transform your Life* is packed full of interesting case studies and creative ideas to boost success. It takes us on a transformative journey through the stress, pain and abuse of our past to areas we can work on for our future, such as enhancing body image, setting goals and having a sense of purpose.

Whether you are new to Matrix Reimprinting or have known its life-changing power since the early days, this book will give you a step-by-step guide to changing core beliefs for yourself or for your clients, whatever the life issue. Finding core beliefs is similar to detective work; clients don't often walk through the door saying, 'I've got a belief that I'm not worthy of true love,' but they may say, 'My relationship is falling apart.' This is why we start with whatever energy is coming up before gently finding and transforming the core belief, which will have undoubtedly seeped into other areas of life as well.

Like Emotional Freedom Technique (EFT), the therapeutic technique that led to Matrix Reimprinting, change with Matrix Reimprinting can be instantaneous, but more often than not it can take systematic work, so we encourage personal practice and include many helpful tips to boost the success of sessions.

Over the last seven years, with the help of his trainers, Karl has taught over 3,000 Matrix Reimprinting practitioners worldwide, including senior psychotherapists, teenagers, doctors, bricklayers, teachers, IT professionals, hairdressers, scientists and counsellors, to name but a few groups drawn to this work. People from all walks of life have come to learn this powerful technique, which integrates the psychoenergetic nature of our reality with the trauma theory of disease and the latest research on the body–mind system. It also draws on traditional talk therapy and inner journeying, and can in fact be likened to parts of over 25 different therapies, ranging from acupuncture to shamanic soul retrieval and Gestalt therapy. You don't need a therapeutic background or a degree in quantum physics to use Matrix Reimprinting, however, just the willingness to learn, to be open to change and to discover new ways of thinking.

How Has Matrix Reimprinting Changed?

For practitioners who are already familiar with the technique, fear not – it hasn't. In fact, it's the opposite: it's been fine-tuned and become simpler in its approach. In *Matrix Reimprinting Using EFT*, several different protocols were outlined; now there is just one.

Karl is confident that this technique, which combines the power of EFT, quantum physics, morphic fields and the Law of Attraction, is now complete. However, we want to stress that the first book is still a must-read for every practitioner, as it offers valuable insights in fields such as addiction, birth, severe trauma and serious disease.

So, how did Karl come to develop Matrix Reimprinting in the first place?

Meet Karl

Karl Dawson is a straight-talking guy who grew up in Bolton in the north of England. His trainees love his down-to-earth approach to energy work. After a pretty normal childhood and school life, he went on to study electrical engineering, but often found himself spending more time in the psychology classes and left after the first year. He worked in a factory repairing pallets for four years and then, at the age of 21, had an internal nagging voice telling him to 'Take a holiday – but go on your own.'

He soon found himself on a beach, where he had a profound spiritual experience. 'It seemed as though I could see deep into the spirit of the people I encountered and share universal truths with them that were previously alien to me.' He had this gift for several months and then suddenly it was gone, leaving a gaping hole in his life. He spent years chasing that deep spiritual connection, desperate to have it back again.

Marriage and two children followed, but as time went by and the marriage broke down, Karl withdrew from life, smoked and drank excessively, and lost his self-confidence and self-value. It's no surprise that his health followed the direction of his esteem, and his lower back, neck and shoulders gave him constant pain. His eyesight deteriorated and he also suffered severe allergies and sensitivities that led to him being tested for bowel cancer. His energy levels were non-existent, and by the time the marriage finally ended, he was sinking into a state of depression. However, after a series of synchronous events, he visited a fasting retreat in Thailand, where he first encountered EFT, or 'tapping'.

As he recalls, 'Over the subsequent months things started to change for the better. My back improved greatly, my need for glasses went away, I had more energy and enthusiasm and my confidence increased.'

Like all deep work, it didn't happen overnight, but over the following few years Karl regained his love of life. Like many others, he wanted to share this great technique and trained as an EFT practitioner and trainer, quickly developing and fine-tuning his skills with hundreds of clients.

In 2006, he passed the rigorous theoretical and practical exams set by EFT creator Gary Craig to become a Founding EFT Master, one of only 29 in the world. He also had the lightbulb moment that led to the development of Matrix Reimprinting and the various protocols that were outlined in *Matrix Reimprinting Using EFT*.

Now Karl has distilled these protocols into one 'Classic' Matrix Reimprinting technique that allows us to understand, accept and change our limiting beliefs and ultimately to create the life we *really* want to live.

Meet Kate

Kate grew up in a leafy London suburb. When she was nine she was awarded a gold star for a story she'd written. At that moment, she decided she wanted to be a writer. Yet even then she felt that in most of her life she wasn't 'good enough' and had a 'bad girl' shadow that followed her around.

Despite the love and affection poured over her by her family, she couldn't shake these feelings and attracted many situations that confirmed her beliefs. By 16 she was self-harming, smoking weed and taking class A drugs most weekends, and writing was confined to manically scribbling in her journal in the midnight hours.

After leaving college she decided on a new dream: she would become a secretary. It took nine months before she realized she wanted to be writing the letters, not typing them up. After a long look in the mirror, she spent the next three years reading English and Media at university; a component of the course was creative writing.

At the end of it, despite gaining a good degree, she still believed she couldn't make it as a writer, so she joined the corporate ranks and spent the next six years selling beer brands to pubs and clubs. For a girl who'd had a dependency on escapism in her teens, alcohol was the next (legal) step. Yet the little nine-year-old still craved recognition for the talent that had made her feel she *was* 'good enough'. Intent on climbing the corporate ladder, Kate resolutely ignored this.

Perhaps this pattern would have continued if it hadn't been for a series of traumatic events in 2009 which gave her the impetus to follow her writing dream, and she grandly headed off to Paris to write a novel. A six-month sabbatical, 60,000 words and a lot of croissants later, however, she still wasn't convinced that she could write, let alone publish the book.

Back at the brewery, Kate was still stuck in a cycle of negative head-chatter when she read the blurb for a different type of writing course: 'Be the Writer You Dream of Being', which promised to examine the emotional side of writing. She signed up immediately.

This was where she encountered EFT. After the first night of tapping she went home a little dazed and said, 'I've tried this weird tapping thing and I feel different somehow – like I believe in myself a little bit more.'

Throwing herself into EFT and Matrix Reimprinting, over the next year she quit her 20-a-day smoking habit, softened the drug use, left the corporate job and launched herself as a freelance writer. Well-known companies signed her up within the first month.

She had woken up, faced her beliefs and wanted to help others do the same, so she trained with Karl in early 2010. Most of the five-day course was spent crying as she faced her past, but over the next three years, alongside running a successful writing business and publishing e-books, she facilitated EFT tapping groups, saw hundreds of clients and ran 'EFT Creativity' workshops. She also credits her son's painless and drug-free birth, 'the most spiritual, joyful and intense event' in her life, to a combination of Matrix Reimprinting, EFT and Hypnobirthing®.

Use This Book Your Way

The first Matrix Reimprinting book sold over 15,000 copies worldwide and was translated into nine languages. Many practitioners have told us that they refer to it constantly. In this book, we offer you an updated resource that shares the latest developments in Matrix Reimprinting, a simplified technique, and the science behind these discoveries.

This book is detailed enough for the psychologist with years of traditional and EFT practice behind them, yet also simple enough for the person new to the world of self-help and Energy Psychology.

You have in your hands a powerful tool which will enable you to explore your own core beliefs and change your thought patterns, which will in turn allow you to harness the full power of the Law of Attraction. And if you can change what you believe and attract into your life, well, you can change anything, including collective consciousness.

We've designed this book so that you can dip in and out of the life areas that you wish to address, but first we ask you to examine your beliefs and your morphic field and, of course, get to know the Classic Matrix Reimprinting Technique.

We invite you to think of this work as tending to your rich inner landscape. The workings of your mind may be viewed as a complex natural environment, with patchwork fields full of flowers, plants and herbs growing alongside winding rivers and fast-flowing streams. This landscape is internally connected, and by tending to a field or building a dam, you will have an effect on the rest of the land. Removing weeds in one area, for example, means they are less likely to spread to another.

Matrix Reimprinting gives you the tools to tend to your inner landscape, a landscape that is alive, growing and changing with every season and every thought you have. You can explore its beauty and plant new seeds of belief where weeds once grew.

As any dedicated gardener will tell you, it takes love, attention and commitment to grow and maintain a healthy garden. Are you ready to grow a lush rainforest in yours?

Part I

THE MAGIC BEHIND MATRIX REIMPRINTING

Chapter 1

THE POWER OF BELIEF

'The greatest revolution in our generation is the discovery that human beings, by changing the inner attitudes of their minds, can change the outer aspects of their lives.'

WILLIAM JAMES

Y our beliefs are the rivers running through the inner landscape of your mind. They are the life source for the fertile soil and affect all that grows there. So, what do you believe about yourself? Do you think you're a good parent? Effective at your job? Clever, rich and talented? Or do you believe you could achieve more in your life? How healthy do you think you are? Do you see the world as a safe place? Is it a world full of love or are you still endlessly searching for romance?

Perhaps this is the first time you've been asked these questions and you aren't sure how to answer. And beliefs are fluid, like water – they shift and change. They create new pathways through our mind, and the more energy that flows into them, the stronger they become. We may find ourselves dealing with torrential rapids.

We all have hundreds of different beliefs about ourselves and the world around us. Some are supportive, some are not. All of them, however, affect our life.

In allopathic medicine, the absolute power of belief systems is shown through placebos, or 'fake medicine'. Placebos don't have to be pills – they can be creams, injections or even surgery – but if we believe in them, they will improve our health. Researchers have measured this by using variables such as colour, dosage and branding. Interestingly, the effect is greater if the dosage is increased. Shiny boxes and a capsule will trump a tablet, and an injection will work even better.[1]

Health authorities are well aware of the placebo effect. According to the UK National Health Service, 'The placebo effect is an example of how our expectations and beliefs can cause real change in our physical bodies. It's a phenomenon that we don't completely understand. But we can see it working in all kinds of ways, and all kinds of circumstances.'[2]

Take this pain-relief study, where a group of students was told that they were going to take part in a study of a new painkiller called trivaricaine. This was a brown lotion that was to be painted on the skin. It smelled medicinal, but contained only water, iodine and thyme oil: it was a placebo. Of course the students were not told this.

The administrator of the 'medicine' donned gloves and a white lab coat. Each student had the trivaricaine painted on one index finger and the other left untreated. Then each index finger in turn was squeezed in a vice.

The students reported significantly less pain in the treated finger. They expected the 'medicine' to kill pain, and sure enough, they experienced less pain. Even though the trivaricaine was a fake painkiller, expectation and belief had produced real results.[3]

This is only one example of hundreds of clinical trials that consistently demonstrate the power of the placebo. Essentially, what we *believe* can make us well. The medical authorities know it too. In March 2013, 783 doctors were polled about their use of sugar pills – a treatment they knew had no medical value – to aid patients' recovery. An overwhelming 97 per cent admitted that they had recommended a sugar pill, and one in 100 gave out these placebos at least once a week.[4]

The power of the placebo is becoming better known in part thanks to Dr Irving Kirsh, a professor at Harvard Medical School. Kirsh challenged the effectiveness of antidepressants, which are worth US$11 billion annually. Following an initial study in 1998, he invoked the Freedom of Information Act and obtained unpublished clinical trial data of antidepressants from American pharmaceutical companies. He found that when these data were included with his original findings, antidepressants outperformed placebos in only 20 of the 48 trials (less than half!) and that the overall difference between drugs and placebos was 'clinically insignificant'.[5] It was the belief in the placebo that directly influenced the subjects and had an impact on their physiology.

Placebo is Latin for 'I shall please.' Just as strong is the opposite term, *nocebo*, meaning 'I shall harm.' If we are told something negative, generally by a person in authority such as a doctor or teacher, it can have just as much power as the placebo, because we totally believe what they are saying. Being told that we have a specific period of time to live or are 'at risk of developing a certain disease', for example, may mean we believe it and so it comes true.

Conversely, there are many documented reports of people who have chosen *not* to believe their medical diagnosis and healed themselves using various techniques, including Matrix Reimprinting.

Where Do Our Beliefs Come From?

So, where do these powerful beliefs come from?

When it comes to understanding how we develop our belief systems, the magic number is six. There are six ways in which we create core beliefs and most of our core beliefs were formed before the age of six.

Why pre-six? Scientific research has now clearly demonstrated that before the age of two our dominant brainwave state is delta, and between two and six it is theta. These brainwaves give a lower electrical energetic reading than those we subsequently use in our waking life. Delta is the slowest frequency, the frequency of deep meditation. Theta is the state that hypnotists drop their clients into in order to make them more suggestible. It is also associated with deep relaxation, creativity, light sleep and dreaming.

Nature cleverly designed us this way because when we are born we don't have any conscious memories – in essence, we are an empty filing cabinet ready to be filled with memories and beliefs – so we enter the world in download mode. It is in our first six years that we form most of our core beliefs and if we encounter any of the following experiences, they are most certainly hard-wired into our subconscious.

Conclusions Based on a Traumatic Experience

When we have a traumatic experience (i.e. when our body goes into fight, flight or freeze mode), we take the conclusions we draw from it into our subconscious so that we can automatically remember them if the situation should present itself again.

After many years of helping people manage their framework of beliefs, we know that beliefs are formed not by trauma itself, but by the conclusions that are drawn from it. For example, if 10 people were to experience the same traumatic event, such as a tsunami, they would all have different beliefs about themselves because of it. Some might believe 'I deserved it', while others might think 'Bad things always happen to me' or 'I'm unlucky.' The same goes for war veterans who were in the same conflict – they will have different beliefs about their time at war. This also explains why some will experience severe PTSD and others will be able to cope well with their time in combat.

Learning Experience

When we have a powerful learning experience, it goes straight to our subconscious so that we don't have to relearn it. Essentially, all our basic skills like walking and talking are compounded learning experiences. Yet we are also continually formulating additional subconscious programs based on new information which has an impact on us.

Post-hypnotic Suggestion

When we are in an altered state of consciousness and a suggestion is made to us, it automatically goes into our subconscious mind. We can be in a hypnotic state like this in the presence of doctors, teachers or anyone who is in a position of power over us and leaves us feeling helpless – which can take us into a post-hypnotic state. This is why it is so important to consider the nocebo effect: the words spoken by 'powerful' people can either support or damage us.

Teaching

We are also in a suggestible state when we are in the role of student. Many people resonate with this point, as they can easily remember times when they were told by teachers that they weren't 'trying hard enough' or were a 'chatterbox' or 'one of the disruptive students'. Add these suggestions to a few school reports which your parents read out to you and you have a traumatic learning and teaching experience rolled into one.

Unconscious Modelling

We learn so much from modelling our parents in the first few years of life. We copy what we see them doing, not what they tell us to do. This continues throughout life (e.g. modelling celebrities or our peers at work), but it is especially potent in those early years, when we are in the theta 'sponge-like' state, as it goes directly into the subconscious database.

Repetition

This is also related to modelling, because if we repeat an action, it goes into the subconscious. This is also why affirmations work over a period of time. Simply repeating a positive affirmation once or twice won't do anything (apart from make us feel a little better at the time), but doing it consistently will change the pathways in our brain, otherwise known as neuroplasticity.

The specialist in this field, Dr David Hamilton, a biochemist, has shown through his research and book *How Your Mind Can Heal Your Body* that every thought we have creates microscopic changes in the structure of our brain. Our neural connections (the communication pathways between our brain cells) become denser when we consistently repeat a specific thought. So, with affirmations, repetition and visualization, our thoughts are changing the physical structure of our brain.[6]

When we understand the importance of the brainwave state in children, together with the six ways in which beliefs go subconscious, it's easy to see why such a strong belief system has grown up around doctors and allopathic medicine. A child gets taken to the doctor when they are feeling unwell (traumatic experience). The doctor is a figure of authority to whom the parent listens attentively (post-hypnotic suggestion and unconscious modelling). The doctor gives the child some medicine and tells them that it will make them better (learning experience). This cycle continues throughout their childhood (repetition). It's no surprise then that the belief system surrounding placebo medicine is one of the strongest and easiest to test.

The Fluidity of Beliefs

Like water, beliefs are fluid – they gather momentum, they shift course, they filter out into new streams. We have core beliefs which branch out and become generalized. They loop backwards and forwards around each other, depending on what is happening in our life at the time.

In 2013, the transformational coach and bestselling author Arielle Essex spoke at the Matrix Reimprinting convention about a client with whom she had been working. Let's call him Lucas. Lucas had been suffering panic attacks and throughout the course of their work together he and Arielle made a visual of his thought loop process between beliefs:

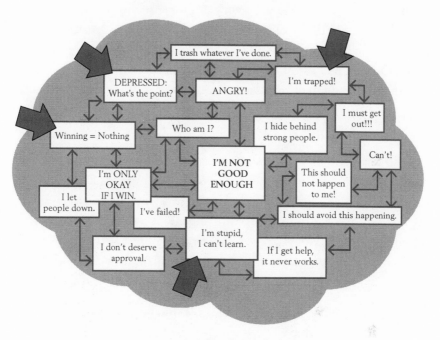

Belief thought loops

Lucas was the eldest son in his family, and his father was the headmaster of his local school and a keen sportsman. He pushed Lucas to succeed both in academia and on the sports pitch. However, Lucas's talents did not lie in either of these areas and he continually felt he let his father down and 'wasn't good enough'. He also found out that his father would often fix little awards so that he would sometimes win one.

Lucas had the belief that 'I'm only OK if I win', along with many other generalizations such as 'I let people down' and 'I'm stupid – I can't learn.' As he grew into a man, he was plagued by self-doubt. On one hand he was desperate to 'win', but on the other, even when he did achieve a goal, he couldn't quite trust it due to his father's 'fixing' during his childhood, so he often felt 'trapped'. These beliefs also brought up strong emotions such as anger, together with a state of depression.

We all have a myriad of beliefs that we've picked up along our journey through life. Yet we aren't often conscious of them until we start looking for them, or they start looking for us. In Lucas's case, he reached the point of having panic attacks and was desperate for some help. Obviously, it's best not to let things get that far. So, where are our beliefs held and how can we access them?

The Two Minds

We all have two amazing and interconnected minds. The one you are using to decipher these words is the conscious mind. It is conscious of itself. It is a creative mind that holds all our wishes and desires. It is not bound by time constraints. Try thinking about a date next week or an appointment a few days ago – your mind will present the information to you in a busy, creative and often image-based way. And this self-conscious mind also gives us the ability to analyse ourselves.

Our other mind is the subconscious. Literally meaning 'below the conscious', it's a database full of programs and beliefs. The conscious mind is wildly creative, while the subconscious is habitual and enables us to function in daily life. This filing cabinet stores all our daily actions from walking to touch-typing, locking doors, brushing teeth or making a phone call. The number of actions that we perform every day runs into the thousands. We couldn't possibly hold all this information in our conscious mind or we'd never get anything done. Imagine having to think about which muscles need to contract, where the pressure needs to go and in what sequence every time we needed to walk. Fortunately, our subconscious mind learned all of this information years ago and stored it in the filing cabinet so it could unconsciously retrieve and use it while we engaged our conscious mind in thinking creatively. All we need now is the intention to walk and our subconscious mind plays that program for us.

The Über-powerful Subconscious Mind

The subconscious mind often gets a bad reputation, but, as the walking example shows, we need it to function in daily life. Scientific research has now proved that in all our daily thoughts, we only use 5 per cent of our creative conscious mind versus 95 per cent of our subconscious mind. Isn't that astounding? It's actually our subconscious mind that is in charge. It's this filing system that is running our life.

What's even more flabbergasting is that scientists have measured cognitive activity and have ascertained that the conscious mind is capable of handling 40 bits of information a second, but the subconscious mind is capable of handling 40 million bits of information a second! So this amazing filing system can absorb 1 million times more information than the conscious mind in a single moment. For example, if you were in a restaurant and someone dropped a glass, your conscious mind would capture 40 pieces of information about that moment, but your subconscious mind would take in 40 million pieces of information, from the smell of the dinner on your plate to the expression on the manager's face, to the clothes you were wearing... and the list goes on.

Staying with a food theme, imagine you are invited to a posh dinner party and lobster is brought out as the main course. You've never eaten lobster before and are intrigued by the strange implements, a claw cracker and lobster pick, that are presented with your dish. You learn how to eat the lobster by nervously asking for advice or watching other diners cracking the crustacean's joints and scooping out the flesh.

A few months later you're attending another dinner party and again lobster is on the menu. At this point you catch your thoughts in slow motion and it is as if they are entering a search term on Google and pulling up the relevant web page, complete with pictures, on how you used the implements at the previous dinner party. This feels like a bridge between the conscious and the subconscious.

So, how about you go on holiday for a week and the resort's speciality dish is lobster and it's on the menu every night? After two or three days, you're a lobster-eating expert. That program is stored in your subconscious and your conscious mind is free to entertain itself with talking to other guests and enjoying the holiday ambience while you are eating lobster. Compare this to the first time you encountered the lobster and your nervousness at the sight of the strange implements.

Add a belief into the mix such as 'I've got to get it right.' This could mean that eating lobster for the first time makes you stressed and nervous. What if you're worried about a potential allergy to shellfish? That will change your experience as well. How about a belief that eating lobster isn't for people like you? Will that influence how you feel about eating the lobster and what you believe other dinner guests might think of your ineptitude with the instruments? So, as well as having these pre-learned programs, your beliefs will underpin how you experience a situation.

It can be quite a daunting thought to know that our conscious mind, the one that holds all our wishes (earn more, be successful, lose weight, etc.) and that we use to make positive affirmations, only has control of 5 per cent of our thoughts. It's also a million times less powerful than our subconscious mind. No wonder it's so hard to change our behaviour and beliefs with willpower and positive affirmations alone – we're trying to do it with the smaller of our two minds.

Beliefs Shape Our Reactions in the World

The face of science has changed over the last decade, with huge advances being made in neuroscience, epigenetics and understanding the role of the heart. These discoveries have shown that what we think and believe changes our physiology right down to our genetic structure. Science is now proving what self-help pioneers like Louise Hay have been teaching for years: that we can heal ourselves. (For easily digestible information on these findings, see *Matrix Reimprinting Using EFT*.)

Quite simply, our body and mind are connected. They work together in a constant flow of messages/energy from cell to cell, and these messages are controlled by signals in both our inner and outer environment. Our inner landscape includes our emotions, our biochemistry, our mental processes and our beliefs. Our outer environment is everything outside ourselves: the external toxins to which we are exposed, the food we eat and the culture in which we grow up. When we encounter a signal from either the inner or outer environment, our body reacts to it by passing messages through our 37 trillion cells. As cellular biologist Bruce Lipton explains,

> *'Cells respond to a massive variety of signals using protein switches: over 100,000 per cell built into its membrane. These protein switches are fundamental units of perception. They read environmental conditions and adjust the biology to meet the need required. This becomes very profound when we own that perception controls behaviour for it is how we perceive the world that controls our lives.'*[7]

If we add the recent discoveries in neuroplasticity into the equation, it's even easier to see that our perception actually alters our brain structure. These findings have shown that the brain is made of a malleable material. When, as a result of physical experiences and/or thoughts, our brain cells (neurons) reach out and make connections with each other, there is a microscopic change in the brain. The more we repeat a thought, the denser the neural connection becomes and the stronger the neural pathway in the brain.

For example, take meditation. Researchers at Massachusetts General Hospital in Boston used MRI scans to document changes in the brain's structure in the areas associated with mindfulness meditation. After eight weeks, the MRI scans revealed an increased density in areas of the brain associated with memory, self-awareness and compassion.[8]

So, the way we react to environmental signals is determined through the filters of our beliefs. Our reactions then change the brain structure: certain neural pathways become deeper and easier for our thoughts to travel down. Great if you're thinking how much you love yourself; not so great if you're constantly doubting your own ability.

Meet Sarah, who has a spider phobia. One morning she is having breakfast in the kitchen before leaving for work when she sees a large spider crawl across the floor. In this instance, the spider acts as the environmental signal and her subconscious mind whips out the pre-learned 'Spiders are dangerous' belief that was imprinted as a result of conclusions drawn from a traumatic experience in the past. This environmental signal and belief then send the message to her cells to act accordingly.

Next comes a whoosh of physiological reactions! The amygdala in Sarah's brain (part of the limbic system controlling our emotions and long-term memory) sends signals to the hypothalamus that it is in danger. The hypothalamus-pituitary-adrenal (HPA) axis is activated, and adrenaline, blood sugars and cortisol are released into the bloodstream.

This in turn can affect a whole host of other bodily functions, such as blood pressure, heart rate, body temperature, blood acidity, intelligence, cognitive ability, stress and anxiety levels and digestion.

In Sarah's case, she is suddenly full of irrational fear of the spider, her breathing is erratic and her hands are shaking as she runs out of the kitchen and locks herself in the bathroom.

Flight, Fight, Freeze

This response has been named 'flight, fight, freeze' and it affects our entire being. We needed it when we were living in caves and found ourselves in genuinely life-threatening situations on a regular basis. It means that mind and body are completely focused, we lose all logic and clarity, and simply want to run or fight. And if we can't run or fight, we freeze.

The freeze response is the least known of the three, but it is important in releasing the trauma or energy of the situation and also in understanding the theory behind Matrix Reimprinting.

We see the freeze response very clearly in the animal kingdom. Trauma specialist Dr Robert Scaer undertook research which involved observing animals in the wild and noting their behaviour during trauma. If you watch an animal being pursued by a predator on TV you will see that when it is chased, it will often collapse and become limp, even before being seized by the predator. This is the freeze response. It is usually a last resort for animals when fight or flight has failed.

When the animal freezes, it releases a flood of endorphins, so that if it is attacked, the pain will be minimized. If the animal is not eaten and survives the period of immobility, in virtually all cases it will begin to tremble. This can range from a shudder to a dramatic seizure.

According to Dr Scaer, slow-motion video of this trembling reveals that it resembles the last act of the animal before it froze – usually the act of running. So the animal generally discharges the freeze response by shaking, breathing deeply and perspiring. After discharging the response, it will emerge unscathed by its ordeal. Dr Scaer theorizes that this is its way of releasing all unconscious memory of the attack.[9] Humans, however, don't do this. In fact shaking after a trauma is seen as a negative symptom and we are often told to calm down.

But why do we go into the fight, flight, freeze response for different external signals? Why is Sarah scared of spiders but other people keep tarantulas as pets? It is due to the beliefs that were imprinted on us by emotional events in the past. In Sarah's case, they are from her childhood, when she watched her mother scream and jump on a chair every time she saw even the tiniest spider. In essence, she was watching her mother become engulfed in the fight or flight response. For a small child, seeing your primary caregiver lose control can be a traumatic experience. Add in the modelling and repetition and you can see why Sarah developed the subconscious belief that spiders are dangerous.

This belief means that every time Sarah sees a spider she will experience an energetic shift in her nervous system into the flight, fight, freeze response, meaning she will respond irrationally to a harmless spider and perhaps spend the next hour full of anxiety behind a locked bathroom door, possibly waiting for someone to rescue her, missing the bus to work and creating further problems for herself. On a conscious level, she knows there is no real threat from the spider, but this energetic reaction in her body will still have her running to the bathroom.

Sarah's personal perception of reality is determined by the beliefs she holds. This does not necessarily make the beliefs real. But her beliefs dictate her attitude to spiders, and her attitude dictates how she responds.

Is there a situation that triggers you into this fight or flight response? What about going on a training course and being asked to stand up and introduce yourself to a room full of strangers? Karl finds this instantly sends the majority of his course attendees into the fight or flight response, as the thought of public speaking strikes fear into people's hearts like nothing else. Many attendees report energy shifts in their body such as a faster heartbeat, dizzy feelings and an instant lump or tightness in the throat at the thought of having to speak in front of a room full of people. These reactions will be based on their beliefs about the safety of public speaking. We wouldn't need to search too far before we came across a previous memory that made them feel unsafe in this situation.

Imagine if Sarah could revisit those times when her mother screamed and her little self was frozen, stuck in fight and flight, and change them. What if we could release the trauma and reimprint those memories so that she and her mother believed spiders were harmless? There's no 'what if' or 'imagine' about it – this is the purpose of Matrix Reimprinting. With it you will learn how to reduce the fight and flight response by exploring the emotional memories in your subconscious mind. You will be able to find the beliefs stored there and elegantly transform them.

Some people intrinsically know what their core beliefs are and how they acquired them, but awareness alone won't transform them. Dr Bruce Lipton sums this up beautifully in his analogy that the subconscious mind is like a CD player playing music from the subconscious database. Simply walking over to the CD player and shouting at it to change the music isn't going to do any good. It's only when we press 'stop' on the player and put on another CD that the music changes. With Matrix Reimprinting we can find our core beliefs and discover when they were hard-wired into our subconscious. We can then reimprint a new belief – a new CD for the player. In this way, Matrix Reimprinting elegantly allows us to release any trapped emotions around a traumatic event and subsequently change a negative core belief into a supportive one.

Your Belief Blueprint

We've seen the power of our subconscious beliefs and how they change our physical and emotional reactions and can be the blueprint for our past and the future. Now, with Matrix Reimprinting you will soon see the connections between your own beliefs and the life events that you have created.

Exercise: Brainstorm Your Beliefs

Your task for this chapter is to 'brainstorm' your beliefs. This will begin to give you a conscious understanding of what they are.

1. Grab some pieces of paper.

2. Look at each of the beliefs on the checklist (*see opposite*) in turn and ask yourself, 'How true is that for me out of 100 as a percentage?' This is known as the 'Validity of Cognition' (VoC) scale.

3. Write down each of the beliefs that rate highly for you in the centre of a new piece of paper.

4. Note your reactions to each belief and create a brainstorm of where they emerge in different areas of your life. List them all, radiating out from the belief in a 'mind map'.

5. Feel free to add your own beliefs.

As you work through this book, you can come back to this map and note down any changes in the validity of your beliefs and any connections that you have made between them and the events in your life.

◆◆◆◆◆

We all have a myriad of beliefs – positive, negative and neutral – and often one core one that we can spend our life proving to be true. There are also shared beliefs that may be culturally or family dependent.

In the next chapter we're going to examine how these beliefs are stored on a personal and human level and how and why our core beliefs form torrential rivers in some parts of our inner landscape and barely make a puddle in others.

Belief	Validity of Cognition – the Truth Percentage
I'm not good enough	
I'm not loveable	
The world is a dangerous place	
I'm worthless	
I'm incapable	
I'm misunderstood	
I'm abandoned	
I'm betrayed	
I'm unattractive	
I'm unproductive	
I'm incompetent	
I'm a failure	
I'm a victim	
I'm a burden	
I'm dumb	
I'm always used	
I'm alone	
I'm bad	
I'm guilty	
I'm sinful	
I'm confused	
I'm trapped	
I'm powerless	

Belief	Validity of Cognition – the Truth Percentage
I'm inferior	
I'm separated from God	

The beliefs checklist

Chapter 2

THE ENERGETIC NATURE
OF OUR UNIVERSE

Quite a big title, huh? Fear not – we're not quantum physicists, and we doubt that many of you are either. There is a sea of information on this fascinating scientific area that you can research to your heart's content if you wish. But you don't need to know any more than what we're going to lay out for you here to understand the energetic nature of our universe, how we tune in to our subconscious mind and how Matrix Reimprinting can change the nature of your own subconscious.

Here are the four concepts that you need to understand:

1. Everything is energy.
2. Energy is organized into fields of information (morphic fields).
3. Our subconscious mind is located in our personal field.
4. We can tune in to these fields of information.

1. Everything is Energy

Pre-seventeenth century, the world was thought to be an evolving organism with a purpose. Then the dawn of mechanistic science brought to the West the belief that nature was mechanical – that all parts of nature were genetically programmed through the structure of their cells. Over time this became a universal belief for many cultures.

However, what quantum physics has now taught us is that the world is composed of electromagnetic energy, which in turn is composed of various atomic and subatomic particles. Underlying our physical world is a vibrational reality – our solid world is in fact an illusion.

Despite the fact that quantum theory is now considered fact and is taught unreservedly in schools, much of modern-day science and medicine is still rooted in the mechanistic view, which, as biologist Rupert Sheldrake explains, 'is brilliant for mechanics, not so good for minds, health and emotional wellbeing'.[1]

So how does this affect us?

Our Energy Body

Due to the electromagnetic nature of the subatomic particles that vibrate and push against each other to form solid structures, we can see that our body is a living, breathing energy system. In the previous chapter we discussed the power of the fight, flight and freeze response, which sets off hundreds of reactions in the body. There is also the emotional reaction.

Consider the word 'emotion', which comes from the Latin conjunction of 'energy in motion'. Our energy is carried around our body through pathways called meridians. We will look at this in more detail later on.

We Reinforce Our Beliefs through Our Vibration

As an energy system, we also have a vibration. This acts like a magnet and attracts a similar frequency. The particular vibration that we are emitting is controlled by our emotions.

In their book *Ask and it is Given*, Esther and Jerry Hicks suggest a scale of 22 emotions that represent the energy – and therefore the vibration – we emit. The spectrum ranges from joy, empowerment and freedom at one end, through optimism and hopefulness, to fear, despair and powerless at the other end of the scale.[2]

Consider the vibration, the weight of the words. Compare 'despair' with 'hopefulness'. If we are continually at the lower end of the scale, that will be the vibration that we are sending out into the world and that we will be attracting back. And as Abraham says, 'By paying attention to the signals of your emotions, you can understand, with absolute precision, everything you are now living or have ever lived.'[3] This is called the Law of Attraction. (If you are new to the concept of the Law of Attraction, we strongly recommend that you watch the film *The Secret* or read Esther and Jerry Hicks' *Ask and it is Given* for an introduction.)

The Law of Attraction also works with our belief systems and explains how they get stronger as we get older, as we are continually attracting events to support what we believe in.

So, if we are holding negative beliefs or programs in our subconscious mind we will be emitting a vibrational signal which attracts negative events to reinforce these beliefs. Fortunately, we can use Matrix Reimprinting to change these beliefs, and therefore our vibrational signal, so that we can begin attracting experiences that we do want.

Sarah's spider phobia is a clear example of a *concise* belief, as phobias often are, but our *core* beliefs are emotionally deeper; for example, 'I'm always wrong' or 'Everyone else is chosen over me.' With core beliefs, we will have had an early experience that has led us to draw a certain conclusion and we will attract life experiences that prove that we are right.

> *Meet Louise. All her life she had been able to attract vast sums of money but hadn't been able to keep hold of them. When she worked with Karl using the Classic Matrix Technique, they traced it back to a five-year-old Louise who'd just done some jobs for her grandma. As a reward, she'd been given a silver dollar, but when her mother had seen it, she'd smacked her and scolded her, saying, 'You don't take money off people.'*

At that moment Louise had concluded that although she could get money, she wasn't allowed to keep it – it was wrong to take money from people.

Louise instantly saw the effect this belief had had on her. Throughout her life she had attracted scenarios where she'd obtained money and lost it again quickly.

Once we understand how the Law of Attraction works, it gives a whole new meaning to positive thinking. We are the creators of our own experiences in life, but this doesn't mean that we accept the blame for anything we're not happy with, nor do we blame anyone else.

Another way of looking at it is that we draw into our life what we need to learn to make ourselves stronger. This is hugely important, as our work is about self-acceptance rather than spending a lifetime 'working' on ourselves and endlessly searching for core beliefs – after all, then the universe would just keep bringing us more stuff to work on!

Over the last decade there have been a plethora of self-help books and gurus stepping forwards and claiming that they can show us how to invoke the Law of Attraction, but we know we have to do this for ourselves. How? We have to find out what is in our energy system in order to see what we are attracting, and to do this, we need to find out what is in our database of stored programs and beliefs, those emotional memories in our *über*-powerful mind, the subconscious.

2. Energy is Organized into Fields of Information (Morphic Fields)

We are all surrounded by fields of information which are invisible to the eye but rich in energetic data. The concept of fields is not a new one – there are already a number of known fields such as the Earth's gravitational field and magnetic fields – but Rupert Sheldrake's work goes one step further and suggests that all living cells, tissues, organs and organisms have their own fields, which he calls 'morphic fields'. These fields shape and form each individual species, and they are also responsible for sociological influences, customs, ways of behaving and habits of the mind.

Nowhere can this be seen more easily than in the animal kingdom. Canada geese know when to migrate; starlings know when to flock together and make beautiful shapes in the sky. Shoals of fish stop and turn at exactly the same point. Communities of ants know when food arrives, simply appearing as if by telepathy, and honey bees innately know their individual roles in the hive.

In the 1920s, Harvard University psychologist William McDougall tested the hypothesis that an organism could pass on to its offspring characteristics that it had acquired during its lifetime. He experimented with rats for over 15 years, testing each new generation's ability to escape from a tank by navigating a maze. The first generation of rats averaged 200 mistakes before they learned the right way out; the last generation only made 20 mistakes.

McDougall concluded that, contrary to accepted genetic science, acquired knowledge could be inherited. In essence, rat families who'd never even been exposed to the maze could tune in to the collective 'rat field' and could run straight through the maze. Evolution doesn't explain this, communication doesn't explain it, the rats' intelligence doesn't explain it, but picking up the collective information through the field does explain it.[4]

We can relate morphic fields in the animal world to how information is passed through the human race. The more a field of behaviour is repeated, the stronger or denser it becomes. We tune in to the fields with which we resonate, and these fields are layered and connected. For the sake of ease, we have organized them into the following areas: universal, cultural, family and personal.

The Universal Field: The Matrix

The largest of these fields is the unified energy field. It's the one that connects us all. Our personal, cultural and family fields are held within this universal energy field, this matrix of energy.

From a religious or spiritual perspective, this isn't a new concept. In fact it pre-dates the Bible and mention of it can be found in every world religion. In essence it is the same as the Akashic records, which are a dimension of consciousness containing a vibrational record of every soul and its journey. The Akashic records are constantly being updated and all information, past, present and future, is held there.

In 1944, Max Planck, whom many consider the father of quantum theory, shocked the world by saying that there was a 'matrix' of energy that provided the blueprint for our physical reality.

In the twenty-first century the concept has been popularized by writers such as Lynne McTaggart and Gregg Braden, together with the films *The Secret* and *What the Bleep Do We Know?*

Various names have been given to this universal field and, as you may have guessed, our preferred name is the Matrix. Whether it's called the field, God, the universe, the divine or indeed the Matrix, we see it as a universe that is conscious of itself and connects us all.

If we are all connected in this way, it follows on that there is no empty space. In *The Divine Matrix*, Gregg Braden challenges the widespread supposition that up to 90 per cent of our cosmos is comprised of empty space:

> *'If it's really vacant, then there's a big question that must be answered: How can the waves of energy that transmit everything from our cell-phone calls to the reflected bright light bringing this page's words to your eyes travel from one place to another? Just as water carries ripples away from the place where a stone is tossed into a pond, something must exist that conveys the vibrations of life from one point to another.'*[5]

It is in this place of pure energy that the vibrations of life are conveyed from one point to another, and it is here that everything begins, from the birth of stars and DNA to our deepest relationships, peace between nations and our own personal healing...

Cultural Fields: Human and Local Culture

The Human Field

As humans, across the world we have one field in common: the human field, the make-up of our physical body. You could also call it the body field. In essence, it's how we develop from one cell to billions of cells that work efficiently as a human form. The question of how this happens has baffled scientists for years. But the idea of the body field explains holistically how our energy system sets what is right for us.

According to biologist Peter Fraser, developmental biologists have 'already found how different body parts have different fields; the brain field is different from the fields that relate to muscles and connective tissues. They've already found the morphic field that relates to the genetic make-up of the body.'[6]

These energetic fields could be the key to understanding how the body regulates itself. How does the body know how to maintain the right temperature, for example? Or what the right blood pressure should be for a specific person? No one knows how this information is stored in the body. Energetic fields would provide an alternative explanation for how our inherent information is organized.

Phantom limb pain is also significant here. A survey has shown that approximately 60 to 80 per cent of individuals with an amputation experience phantom sensations in their amputated limb, and the majority of the sensations are painful.[7] It is the brain that is making the connection – it is tuning in to that limb's morphic field.

All the information about the body, from the level of a cell to a whole human being, is contained in layered fields that are holistic, part of each other. For example, legs would have a field of information that not only contained their physical make-up, what cells were in them, how they worked, etc., but also information that stretched out beyond the personal to how, say, legs were viewed in a sexual context by that culture's field. Essentially, there is information about the purpose and meaning of body parts in each of their fields.

The Human Field of Fear

One aspect of being in a human body is having the fears that come with it. The minute we come from spirit to consciousness, we experience fear. The moment we are born we have three basic fears: 1) fear of the dark; 2) fear of falling; and 3) fear of being alone.

Are these our fears or the fears of the millions who have come before us? Fear does seep down through generations. If a family connects to a particular fear and makes it their own, it will continue throughout the family line. We can also look at this another way; powerful families or dynasties remain powerful because they don't tune in to that field of fear, of lack, of separation.

The majority of us on this planet live in fear, however, and the fears are layered upon each other several times over. Fear seeps into everything we do: fear that we won't pass our exams, or get a job, or find a partner – that in essence we will be separate, alone, cast out. Think of this field of fear as a huge melting-pot with people constantly adding to it. The result is long-established doctrines that are never questioned or challenged. For example, our lifespan. If you had told someone 300 years ago that the average life expectancy was 75 years, they would have said, 'That's preposterous – people die at 50.'

We want to show you how, using Matrix Reimprinting, we are changing the morphic field of fear on both a personal and an evolutionary level.

Local Cultural Fields

When you look at the cultural layer of a national field or an area's local customs, you can easily see how fields of behaviour can build up and how they can change over time.

Karl has travelled extensively to teach Matrix Reimprinting and is always fascinated by the cultural fields in different countries – the way that cultures are uniquely themselves, from appearance to belief systems. In Japan, for example, he noticed that there was an inherent sense of responsibility, while in some Middle Eastern countries it could be said that the lack of equal rights for women is as much a cultural field as a political doctrine.

Once you understand fields of behaviour, you see them everywhere and how they have changed over the decades. If we look at the UK and the USA since the turn of the twentieth century, we can see changes in fashion, language, music and work that were all met with resistance initially, but eventually became mainstream. For example, in the 1960s and 1970s, ideas around free love, drug-taking and dress sense were initially only part of a subversive culture, yet drugs are now commonplace and fashion is a post-modern mix of everything that has gone before. Compare a female pop star's clothing from the 1980s to that of 2013 and you can see how even in this space of time the fields of fashion have changed. Tattoos and body piercings, for example, were once only seen on punks, sailors and bikers, yet now are found in all areas of society. Even with language, swearwords that were frowned on 50 years ago are now part of the common tongue.

Once new behaviour comes up and a field is built around it, there is initial resistance from society, then the numbers adding to that field reach critical mass and it becomes mainstream.

Family Fields

As we narrow down our fields from culture to our immediate environment, one of the strongest is our family field. We have strong morphic resonance with those who are most like us, and our family is genetically the closest both from a DNA and a self-receptor perspective. We can all relate to being like our parents or seeing our personality traits or habits in our children.

> Meet Christy, who had suffered from depression all her adult life. When she went into the Matrix, she met her two-year-old self, who was sitting outside her mother's bedroom, scared to be with Mum when she felt depressed.

> When the negative emotions had been cleared, her mother explained that she had learned this behaviour from her own mother and brought Grandma into the scene.

> When the underlying pattern had been cleared, eventually all three generations sat together in a state of peace.

This is so common when working with Matrix Reimprinting and shows how we learn our beliefs and patterns of behaviour from those around us. We spend the first six years downloading information, and who is in our awareness at that time? For most of us, it is our parents.

But how do our children pick up our habits if they've had no conscious exposure to the behaviour? For example, when Karl was in his twenties he worked in a bar and would often practise his cocktail-making skills by throwing bottles in the air and catching them before pouring exotic-looking drinks. Fast-forward 20 years and Karl is visiting his 18-year-old son, Daniel, at his new bar job and watching in amazement as he is spinning the bottles in the air with the same accuracy that Karl had two decades earlier. Karl has never shown Daniel how to spin bottles or pour cocktails – he's never even mentioned it. Is it simply coincidence that Daniel can do it or has Daniel picked up this skill from his father's field?

Just as our beliefs go into our subconscious through modelling, repetition and trauma, we tune in to our family's field of behaviour without being consciously aware of it. We pick up belief systems that may have been passed down through many generations – and may no longer be useful to us.

Personal Fields

Personally, we all have inherent instinctive behaviour. We all know to suckle at our mother's breast when we are born, for example. Learned behaviour is different and becomes established through repetition, therefore making the morphic field stronger. Put another way, the more energy in the field, the stronger the field becomes.

Take someone with a rat phobia. Rats are quite easy to avoid, so it's unlikely that the phobia will be triggered constantly, therefore the morphic field of behaviour around it won't be particularly dense. This doesn't mean that the phobic reaction isn't intense, just that there will be fewer instances when it is triggered. There isn't a lot of repetition within that particular field. This means that the energy can be cleared quickly with Matrix Reimprinting, often in one session.

However, if you look at obsessive compulsive disorder (OCD) and the ingrained habits that are intrinsic to the condition, whether turning on light switches, washing hands or repeating certain words, they will have a very strong morphic field around them due to the amount of repetition. Therefore it will often take sustained work to clear that personal field of that energy.

3. Our Subconscious Mind is Located in Our Personal Field

Linked to our personal field is the question of the location of our subconscious mind. We've discussed how our memories are stored in our subconscious mind, but where is our subconscious mind itself stored?

We believe that our subconscious mind isn't kept in our brain but outside our physical body. It's part of our personal field and therefore part of each layer above it, including the universal Matrix that connects us all.

There is much to suggest that memory (the part of the subconscious mind with which we are concerned here) is not stored in the brain. Orthodox medical theory has for some time assumed that memory and habits are stored as 'material traces' in the brain. However, countless experiments have been performed to attempt to prove this and none has been successful.[8] Also, according to neuroscientist Francis Crick, there is a practical issue with the idea that memory is stored in the brain. Human memory often lasts decades. Yet it is believed that, with the exception of DNA, nearly all the molecules in our body turn over within days, weeks or months. Memory cannot, therefore, be stored in the brain, as the brain also experiences this molecular turnover.[9]

We can also tune in to our field of information quickly and pull up something from the database. We can even tune in to other people's fields and read their information. This goes some way to explain how intuition and telepathy work.

Dr Bruce Lipton has led the way in our understanding of how we tune in to these fields and to our subconscious mind. He is an inspiring speaker and author, and we will paraphrase him here:

> 'The memory is not in the cell, it is in the field. We are a broadcast – the body is a television set. We have antennas. When the picture tuning breaks on the TV, what do we say? The TV is dead. But did the broadcast stop? No. How can you tell? You get another TV set and you plug it in, turn it on and tune it to the station. When you hit that frequency, boom, it's back on again.
>
> We are immortal. We don't live in the system. We don't live in the TV set.
>
> I asked myself, "If I live 'out there' then why live in the body at all?" The answer I received from my cells was "If you are just a spirit, what does chocolate taste like? What does a sunset look like? What does being in love feel like?"

Why is that relevant? It's the cells that take that environmental information and convert it into an awareness that I can understand. The real world is converted into electromagnetic vibrations. I'm reading the energy, I'm not reading the chemistry, I'm not physically seeing the light, I'm reading the energy of all of that.

My physical body is a device to sense the world. It's a device to come in here to create a world. If anyone has the fondest idea of a heaven and they're looking elsewhere, I think it's a great mistake. The opportunity was to come here and create right here what you thought you'd create in heaven. If it looks like hell, it's because you bought other people's creations.

You have the opportunity to create your own life. I didn't know that as a cellular biologist, but when I owned it as a man, when I caught hold of those limiting beliefs that I made in the first six years, the ones that say, "You can't heal yourself, you aren't smart enough, good enough," I understood it. If you eliminate those beliefs and have a blank slate, you can create anything on this planet, including that dream you thought heaven was. You can create heaven on Earth."[10]

4. We Can Tune in to these Fields of Information

So, our subconscious mind, including all of our memories, is in the field and is part of the Matrix. It contains all the programs and beliefs that we've learned in life, often when we were in the downloadable state pre-six years of age. How do we access it?

Try and remember a time you felt frightened. You will be presented with a picture. You may have a tendency to be more visual, auditory or kinaesthetic when seeing this picture – the emphasis may be on seeing, hearing or feeling it – yet it will be an image all the same. The language of our subconscious is images and this is how the information from the field is communicated to us.

These images are pulled up every time we receive an environmental signal. On a subconscious level they are live memories happening now. They are extremely powerful, as they are our belief filters, the way in which we read the energy around us, which means they ultimately control our reactions, our emotions and our physiology. Karl sees this process as flipping a switch or turning off a tap – the information comes in from the energy field, creating signals that we pick up either energetically or physically, and our body reacts accordingly with a pre-programmed response. We believe that any disruption of the body's energy system can be traced back to disruptive images held in the Matrix.

In Matrix Reimprinting we enter the matrix by working with the pictures we have stored in our energetic database and we can communicate with the younger parts of ourselves, whom we call ECHOs (energetic consciousness holograms). (You will learn more about them in Chapter 5.)

With Matrix Reimprinting, we are consciously exploring what is held in our personal Matrix, releasing lower-vibrational emotions and reimprinting the Matrix with higher-vibrational emotions and pictures.

When we understand the Law of Attraction, the role of the Matrix, and our complex make-up of fields, neural pathways and subconscious memories, it's easy to see why the Law of Attraction might not be working so well for us: because 95 per cent of our daily thoughts and actions are coming from the subconscious mind. The stuff we consciously want, whether it's a new partner, shiny red car, money or happiness, isn't appearing because we're getting what we subconsciously believe instead!

When it comes to beliefs, it's exactly the same principle: we attract the same vibration as the belief we hold. We create events around that belief because we're constantly looking for proof that it's right. We see our beliefs everywhere we look, projecting them onto other people as well as ourselves. We could have a whole lifetime of events that prove we're not clever, not lovable, not worthy, not safe. In the next chapter you'll read how Diana's life was underpinned by one belief that affected her relationships, career, health and family life.

When we get specific and drill down to our core belief, we'll see how it flows into every area of our life. And by releasing the intensity of the beliefs that don't serve us, we'll no longer need to create events that prove them to be right. It is this sustained work that changes our point of attraction in the universal Matrix, thus changing what we attract into our life. As Bruce Lipton said, when we remove those limiting beliefs, we can create heaven on Earth.

Chapter 3
THE JOURNEY OF ONE BELIEF

Meet Diana, a lady in her late forties suffering from general anxiety, depression and IBS and taking medication for all three. This is the story of her belief that 'When everything is going well, when people are happy, I'll screw it up for everyone.' It began as a spring, high up in the mountains of her childhood. The rainwater that was left from the traumas she encountered then formed tiny channels. As more water entered the channels, they grew into gullies flowing into each other, and eventually, as more water rained down, they became big enough to form a river. This river of belief grew into a torrent of fast-flowing water ever-present in all aspects of Diana's life.

Diana's story

It's Christmas Eve and a new baby girl, Diana, has been born. At home the family waits anxiously under the twinkling lights of the Christmas tree. Under one of those lights, the baby's older sister kicks a present. No one is paying any attention to her, no one cares about her presents or leaving out the mince pie for Santa. Her father calls over to her, 'Wow, your baby sister is extra-special, because she's been born on Christmas Eve. We'll go and visit her soon.'

Later, in the hospital ward, when all the big sister can think about is the pile of presents at home, she peers down into the scrunched-up face of her new baby sister. She dislikes her already. 'What's so special about being born at Christmas? She's ruined it for me.'

At that moment, baby Diana believes that she has messed up Christmas. She also takes on the belief 'I am responsible for making my sister happy.'

Fast-forward 48 years. It's Christmas 2011 and inside, Diana is crumbling. She knows she has to carry on getting through the days at work, as she has two daughters to support. Her husband has lost his job, and she is working as a full-time PA and is already reliant on medication for anxiety and depression.

Just before Christmas she gets a promotion at work and becomes PA to the MD of the company. The new job results in even more stress being piled on her already overloaded system and she can't take it any more. When she finally finishes work for the Christmas break, she falls to a new level of anxiety that constantly gnaws at her.

It is at this point that she begins work with a Matrix Reimprinting practitioner to see where all this 'anxiety' has come from. These are some of the memories they discovered on their journey together to the core belief that started when Diana was born.

Early Childhood

Following the energy of the anxiety, which feels like 'a weight of responsibility in her gut', the first memory that emerges for Diana is when she is five years old and sitting on her bed. Her bedroom is dark and she doesn't quite know why she's gone to this picture, but she turns the light on and communicates with her five-year-old ECHO.

Little Diana tells her that she is worried about visiting Grandma the next day. She believes that Grandma doesn't love her and that her extended family don't like her much either. She has the feeling that she's letting her mum down because of this. Everyone else in the family is happy to be visiting Grandma, but she feels that she's ruining it for everyone.

Next Diana visits a picture where she is two years old and playing in the garden. She smiles. 'It's a nice memory. I don't know why I'm here.' But then she steps into the memory to see what it's about and *sees her ECHO walking into the swing, which hits her on the head. Her mum comes rushing out and berates her older brother and sister for not watching out for her. The afternoon has been ruined and Diana believes she has spoilt it for everyone once again.*

School Memories

At school, Diana was really sporty and loved playing hockey. In one memory she was doing trials for the county when she had an accident with the ball that embarrassed her in front of her team-mates so she decided that she didn't want to play again. This meant that she got into a lot of trouble with the sports teacher, who was very angry at her for 'letting the team down'.

Diana also liked running and was in the school relay team. They were a good team but kept messing up in the actual race. Diana ran the third leg and she could never hand the baton to the girl in the fourth leg. Even though it was always the other girl's fault, as she took off too soon, Diana took on that responsibility and felt that she had let the whole side down.

Adulthood

In her late thirties, Diana became pregnant. Her whole family was extremely happy for her. Sadly, the baby died and she had to carry it for a week before giving birth. Understandably, she was traumatized by this event. She and her husband were living on the south coast of England at the time and eventually moved back up to the Midlands, but Diana went back to visit the baby's grave obsessively every weekend.

Again she felt that when everyone was happy, she'd 'screwed it up for them', because it was her fault that she'd lost the child. She believed that she'd lost the baby because she'd chosen to have an abortion in her late teens.

In one of her earlier jobs, she'd worked in a bank. She'd loved the job and loved the people she'd worked with. One day, however, she'd made a mistake which meant the books didn't balance. The whole team had to stay behind until they found out where the missing money was, and eventually they found that it was Diana's fault. From that day onwards she went into work with a huge sense of dread, a weight of responsibility and anxiety in her stomach. This experience was another contribution, another gully of water that added to her ongoing problems with anxiety and depression.

Added to this was that she later got divorced and felt that she had to be emotionally and financially responsible for both her daughters.

It's now 2014, and through being consciously aware of the core belief that has been running her life and being able to clear old traumas and patterns using Matrix Reimprinting, Diana has seen her life transformed. Many of the individual sessions were intensely powerful. Diana 'felt huge shifts and that weights had been lifted', yet it also took commitment and consistency to change the fields of behaviour confirming her belief. As you've read, it started from birth, and she attracted situations to confirm it throughout school and adulthood. Clearing it has been a three-year process. As with all deep work and realignment, the changes have been gradual, but they have all added up.

Diana no longer takes any medication and she is able to socialize, whereas before she would avoid social occasions 'to avoid spoiling them for everyone else'. There is still some anxiety and a slight fear of messing up, yet these run at normal levels and her job as a PA has meant that she has set herself up to be in situations where she is constantly responsible for other people's lives on an organizational level.

Diana has transformed her core belief and changed her point of attraction so that she is attracting more positive things into her life. She now sees herself as a good mother, allows herself to take holidays, and a close friend has remarked that 'the vitality is back – she has got a shine in her eyes'. Most importantly, she is no longer looking for proof that when things are going well, she will screw it up for everyone.

Chapter 4

FROM EMOTIONAL FREEDOM TECHNIQUE TO MATRIX REIMPRINTING

Type in to Google 'Emotional Freedom Technique', 'EFT' or 'tapping' followed by an emotional or physical problem with which you're struggling and you'll soon be reading testimonials of clients who've used this technique to aid their recovery. The popularity of EFT is also testament to its efficacy, with over 500,000 people attending the Tapping World Summit online in 2014. Leaders in the self-help field such as Louise Hay, Jack Canfield and Wayne Dyer amongst others are all using tapping and encouraging us to try it.

It isn't just the self-help world that has embraced EFT – there is now an ever-growing body of research that proves it has a positive effect on people as well as scientifically rewiring the brain, and in the process, rewiring belief systems.

Matrix Reimprinting evolved from Emotional Freedom Technique and the process of tapping is one of its four underlying principles. You will need to know basic EFT to use Matrix Reimprinting and if you want to become a Matrix Reimprinting practitioner then you will need to be trained to Level 2. In this section, we are going to outline what tapping is and how to carry out the two main basic protocols.

How Does It Work?

Tapping is based on the same theory as Chinese acupuncture: that our body has a pathway of energy channels called meridian lines which carry energy through our system. Through the work of Dr Roger Callahan and Gary Craig we now know that tapping on the ends of these meridians (which correlate to specific organs in the body) reduces the fight or flight response, whether the trigger is real or imagined.

> *Meet Samantha. When she was 15 she was attacked by a man who had red facial hair. Afterwards, every time she saw a man with red facial hair, her body would go into the fight or flight response. If she was walking down a road and a man with red facial hair came towards her, she would shake. Red facial hair meant danger and the energy in her body changed accordingly.*

In essence, with tapping, we verbally and energetically tune in to an issue – emotional, physical, mental or spiritual – and tap on several different acupoints on the body whilst repeating a reminder phrase about the issue. This then reduces the fight or flight signal from the brain and results in emotional and cognitive shifts.

In this way, EFT brings together the ancient wisdom of the East about the energy of the body and modern psychology and neurology. Hence the umbrella term 'Energy Psychology'.

Finding it hard to believe that tapping on your body can release energetic trauma? Well, it's now confirmed by scientific research from Harvard Medical School. Over the last decade, researchers there used MRI and PET scans to prove that tapping decreases activity in the parts of the brain associated with fear (amygdala, hippocampus etc). In their research, it's easy to see the amygdala's red alert being called off when acupoints are stimulated.[1]

There are now over 55 published and peer-reviewed studies showing the efficacy of EFT and other Energy Psychology modalities on a variety of issues, including anxiety, athletic performance, depression, pain, physical symptoms, PTSD and weight loss.[2]

You can read more about the scientific evidence for Matrix Reimprinting in the two studies quoted in the appendix, 'The Evidence behind the Matrix Magic'. In addition, Karl and Sasha covered the history and efficacy of TFT and EFT in *Matrix Reimprinting Using EFT*, and you may also wish to refer to this.

The Basic Tapping Technique

Tapping works in three ways:

1. The basic tapping technique protocol reduces the physical or emotional symptoms in the body and turns off the fight or flight response.
2. When the underlying issues or traumatic memories that are causing the response present themselves, EFTers use the Movie Technique (*see p.50*) to remove all the negative aspects of that memory, which in turn resets that particular pre-programmed response.
3. Beyond the traumatic incident and the clearing of the responses are the belief systems that are in place, and this is where Matrix Reimprinting really shines and takes the potential of EFT even further.

The basic tapping technique is relatively easy to learn, but takes practice to master.

Tapping Basic Protocol

Tapping is a practical tool. You won't understand it by simply reading these words – you have to have physical experience of it. So, what are you waiting for?

Step 1: Select the Problem

Find a problem that you want to feel better about. It may be either physical or emotional. Tune in to how that issue is making you feel physically – are you feeling nausea in the gut, a tightness in the throat, a pricking at the back of the eyes? Find the location of the issue in the body – the shape, the colour, the weight, the sensation.

Step 2: Rate the Problem out of 10

It's important to be able to measure your emotions, so that you know when they have shifted or changed. We use the Subjective Units of Distress (SUDS) scale between 0 and 10, with 0 being 'not a problem' and 10 being 'as intense as it gets'.

For some people, giving a measurement is easy; others find it hard to translate emotions into numbers. Our favourite question/reframe for people who can't grasp a number is: 'If you did know the number, what would it be?' or, to put it another way, 'Just guess the number that comes up.' The subconscious mind will present what's right.

Step 3: The Set-up Statement

The set-up is a way of overcoming any resistance to change. We have to accept where we are before we can move through it. A good set-up:

✧ says hello to the problem

✧ finds the words that resonate with us

✧ is specific

Imagine saying 'hello' to someone and shaking hands. The fleshy part of your hand where their fingers grip is called the karate chop point. It is in line with the little finger. In the set-up, you are shaking hands with the problem, so you tap on this point whilst saying the set-up phrase out loud, which is:

'Even though I [have this problem], I love and accept myself.'

Always replace the words 'have this problem' with the specific symptom or issue you are working on, the one you outlined in Step 1.

It's also important to know the difference between global and specific statements, as the more specific you are, the more success you will have.

- ✦ Global: 'Even though I'm feeling depressed…' versus specific: 'Even though I'm feeling this black heaviness in my heart…'
- ✦ Global: 'Even though I'm poor…' versus specific: 'Even though I have no money in my bank account…'
- ✦ Global: 'Even though I have no time…' versus specific: 'Even though I feel overwhelmed by the amount of work I have to do…' (or, even better, tune in to how that feeling of being overwhelmed is expressed in the body).

The more specific you are about the thought, feeling, emotion or energetic disturbance, the more success you will have. For example:

- ✦ 'Even though I have this yellow drippy gurgling in my stomach, I love and accept myself.'
- ✦ 'Even though I have this blue ice gripping my heart, I love and accept myself.'

Repeat the set-up phrase while continuing to tap on the karate chop point. This should diffuse the energy around any resistance to change.

Please note you can alter the wording of the set-up statement to suit yourself. Some people use 'totally love and accept myself', others prefer 'deeply and profoundly love and accept myself' and some people have a hard time saying any of these words and go for 'I can choose to love myself in this moment' or simply 'I'm OK.' It's important to find the words that feel true and natural to you. Honour your differences.

Step 4: A Reminder Phrase

You need a reminder phrase that is a shortened version of your set-up statement. If your set-up was 'Even though I have this blue fear in my heart, I love and accept myself anyway', your reminder phrase would be 'blue fear in my heart'.

Step 5: Tapping

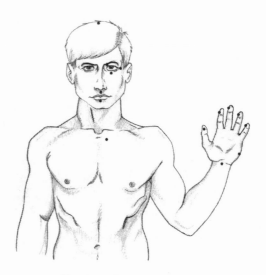

Tapping points

As you can see in the diagram, there are several points on which you will be tapping:

✧ *Top of the head (TH):* On the crown of your head with the flat of your fingers.

✧ *Inside the eyebrow (IE):* Just up and across from the nose.

✧ *Side of the eye (SE):* On the bone around the side of the eye.

✧ *Under the eye (UE):* On the bone under the eye, about two and a half centimetres (an inch) below the pupil.

- *Under the nose (UN):* The small hollow above the lip.

- *Under the lip (UL):* Under the bottom lip, midway between the point of the chin and the bottom of the lower lip.

- *Collarbone (CB):* Find your collarbone and locate the 'U' shape at the top of your breastbone, where a gentleman's tie knot would sit. At the bottom of the 'U' shape, move your fingers out two and a half centimetres (one inch) until you find a slight dent on either side. These are your collarbone points.

- *Under the arm (UA):* Around 10cm (4in) below the armpit. This point is approximately in line with the nipple for men and the bra strap for women.

- *Wrist (WR):* Across the inside of your wrist.

- *Thumb (TH):* With your palm towards you, on the nearside corner of your thumbnail.

- *Index finger (IF):* With your palm towards you, on the nearside corner of your index fingernail.

- *Middle finger (MF):* With your palm towards you, on the nearside corner of your middle fingernail.

- *Ring finger (RF):* With your palm towards you, on the nearside corner of your ring fingernail.

- *Little finger (LF):* With your palm towards you, on the nearside corner of your little fingernail.

Start at the top of your body and work down the points. Tap five to seven times with two fingers on each point, using a soft therapeutic touch whilst saying the reminder phrase.

With the exception of the points under the nose or on the chin, the tapping points are on both sides of the body. You can use your left or right hand, and it doesn't matter if you tap on either side of the body or on both sides at once. It is also OK to change sides, and if one point feels really good, feel free to stay there a while. It's your body, so give yourself permission to try it out in the way that feels right for you. Protocols are there to guide us, that's all; you will eventually find your own way of tapping within the structure of the protocol.

Step 6: Reassess the Intensity of the Problem

At the end of the round of EFT, you need to check whether the problem has changed or moved. Check the SUDS level (score out of 10) to see if the intensity of your symptoms has changed. What number is it now? Has the colour changed? Has it moved to a different area of the body? Has the intensity gone up?

Step 7: Subsequent Rounds

Continue with subsequent rounds until the problem is down to a zero.

If you are working with the same symptoms, you won't need to carry out the set-up phrase for each round. But if the symptoms begin moving around the body and you start working on something new (from a blue fear in the heart to a tightness in the throat, for example), you'll need a new set-up phrase.

This is known as 'chasing the pain' and it's exactly what the title suggests: you simply chase the pain around the body and change the set-up statement each time. For example, a pain in the shoulder might feel like 'blue ice', then after one round it could have changed to 'red searing pain under the arm'. Keep chasing it around the body and doing new rounds of basic EFT until the symptoms come down to zero and the pain has gone.

If you're focusing on an emotional issue rather than chasing the pain, look out for cognitive shifts where the intensity of the problem has lifted. Often these come in the form of:

✧ 'It's over.'

✧ 'It's gone.'

✧ 'I can't feel it any more.'

✧ 'I'm safe.'

✧ 'I can let go now.'

✧ 'I feel OK about that issue.'

Step 8: Challenge the Results

Once the problem or feeling is down to zero and there are no more physical or emotional symptoms, try hard to imagine the original emotion or pain, so that you can clarify that the process has worked for you. Dig deep to tune in to the feelings and if there is no intensity left then you know that part of the original problem has disappeared.

Step 9: Persist

If the problem remains after the results have been challenged, persist until it is zero (or a very low level) on the SUDS scale.

We suggest that you try out the basic EFT protocol on a few issues so that you become familiar with the tapping points and how energy feels in your body.

Remember we said that there were three ways in which EFT worked? This is the first stage: clearing symptoms in your body and releasing any stuck energy.

The second stage is to find the memories that underpinned the symptoms in the first place. Perhaps you can already think of memories that you'd like to feel differently about or perhaps memories have surfaced while you've been tapping – or even just a whiff of a memory. For example, if you're working on anxiety, a memory may surface that includes your dad shouting at you when you were nine. These memories are important and hold the key to why you're feeling that anxiety in the first place. The further back you can go in your childhood, the more likely that you'll chance upon a core event where this pattern or belief started.

This is why, after you've tuned in to the energy in your body, your next question should always be: 'What is the earliest memory this goes back to?'

Once you have a memory, you can use the EFT Movie Technique, which is outlined below.

Big 'T' and Little 't' Traumas

First, however, we'd like to take a moment to discuss big 'T' and little 't' traumas. All of us will have a mix of these and it is our perception of whether a trauma is big or little that's important. Two people could be involved in the same event but categorize it differently. Perception is everything. Belief is everything.

When you select a memory to work with, think about how 'big' that trauma was for you. Was it a life-or-death scenario? Were you being abused in some way? Or was it when the teacher shouted at you for being late? Rate your SUDS levels and explore the differences. We strongly advise that for big 'T' traumas you work with a trained EFT/Matrix Reimprinting practitioner, as you may experience overwhelming emotions that you may not be ready to deal with on your own.

Using the EFT Movie Technique

1. The Memory
Identify a specific memory. It needs to be a single event.

2. Movie Length
How long will the movie last? The event needs to have spread over time, from a minimum of a couple of minutes to a maximum

of 20 minutes in real time, within a single morning, afternoon, evening or night. If it spans a longer period, break it into several separate movies.

3. Movie Title

What will the title of the movie be? For example, *Dad Shouting*. It only needs to be a word or two.

4. Assess Your SUDS Level at the Movie Title

Check your SUDS level (intensity out of 10) at the movie title. Take the edge off the intensity with: 'Even though I have this *Dad Shouting* movie, I love and accept myself.'

Do this until you can say the title and the intensity has reduced to no more than two to four.

5. Narrate the Movie

Start the movie before there is any emotional intensity. Narrate it out loud, stopping at any points of intensity and resolving them with the EFT protocol.

As different aspects come up in the movie, use the same process until all the aspects have cleared. Each memory is likely to have a host of aspects attached to it and you can use EFT to tap on the symptoms. Think of a cat phobia, for example. What does it consist of? It might be the way a cat purrs, the way it looks at you, the way it curls around your leg, the feeling that it might pounce on you at any minute... Within the movie you can tap on each of these aspects or symptoms to reduce their intensity as you move through the memory.

6. Check Your Work

When you've finished, run the movie again in your mind, checking you've resolved the intensity. If there are any aspects that you've missed or that still have some intensity, tap in the normal way.

Then replay the movie really vividly. Again, tap on any remaining aspects if there is still some intensity.

The technique is complete when you can play the whole movie without any intensity.

◆◆◆◆◆

Multiple Memories and Brainstorms

The issue may have been created by a single life experience or memory. However, most issues are complex and multiple memories will underpin them. Often we have to resolve a number of these memories to achieve resolution of the main issue. This is how belief systems become compounded in the first place.

If we add the concept of morphic fields into the mix, we can see that some issues will have a much denser field of behaviour and lots of memories associated with them. Because we are vibrational beings and attract similar situations into our reality, this in turn will cause our issues to become even more complex, as we add programs to the subconscious filing system. It is likely that there'll be lots of life experiences related to the same theme or belief. As we explore Matrix Reimprinting, we'll be able to connect the dots and realize how we've attracted situations into our life that prove our beliefs to be true.

Brainstorm the Main Issue. What Is It for You?

Start tapping on a memory or the thought, feeling and emotion associated with it and continue until you feel differently about it. Don't worry – you won't need to tap on every single memory related to it! Go for the ones that you feel most emotion about and if you clear enough of these then the little traumas won't bother you so much. You'll collapse the problem. This is called 'the generalization effect'.

◆◆◆◆◆

Now you have the two main techniques within EFT. EFT is one of the founding principles of Matrix Reimprinting. Turn the page and learn the remaining three and how working in the Matrix advances the power of EFT.

Chapter 5

THE FOUR PRINCIPLES OF MATRIX REIMPRINTING

After familiarizing yourself with the EFT protocol and the Movie Technique, you'll easily see how the subconscious mind works – it will search for memories or pictures that underpin the issue that you want to clear.

Matrix Reimprinting goes one step further than EFT because rather than simply watching a movie of a memory, you actively play a part in it. It doesn't leave an empty file where the memory once was – it creates a harmonious picture instead. Imprinting this on your subconscious mind will flood your system with positive energy and beliefs every time you pull it up. It will change your point of vibration and you'll begin to attract positive situations.

You don't need a degree in quantum physics or psychotherapeutic training to learn Matrix Reimprinting. There are only four core principles to the technique:

✧ *ECHOs (Energetic Conscious Holograms):* How we store our trauma in the subconscious

✧ *Tapping:* How we can release trauma using tapping

✧ *Our role as practitioner:* How we create new trauma-free supportive pictures for others

✧ *The role of the heart:* How we release this information into the Matrix

Principle 1: ECHOs

By now you'll have an idea of what some of your beliefs might be. Think of a belief and a time when that belief was true for you. For example, if your belief is 'The world is a dangerous place', you might remember when you had a car accident 10 years ago. That younger you in the car accident is your ECHO, an Energetic Conscious Hologram reverberating in the Matrix.

On one level, the word 'echo' has many connotations: a sound that reverberates beyond our control, a repetition that is distorted and a noise that we can't see but know is present. It also has a magical quality to it. Imagine shouting down a tunnel and then listening to that elusive echo, your voice eerily repeating into space. For all of these reasons, the term 'ECHO' fits well with Matrix Reimprinting, and many people who don't want or need to know the science behind the name are satisfied with the term to describe the younger part of themselves.

The concept of 'parts' is not new. In traditional counselling and psychotherapy, parts are often described as 'inner children'. The idea also features in the process of soul retrieval in shamanism. Many therapies conclude that when we experience a trauma, part of us splits off to protect us from the trauma, dulling or blocking our memory of the event. At the same time, a part of us relives the trauma over and over again, below the threshold of conscious awareness, as if it had never really ended.

The ECHOs Hold the Trauma

An ECHO is a part of us that is below conscious awareness, part of our personal field. As we know, when we experience a trauma, if we can't fight or take flight, we freeze. An ECHO is the part of us that has split off and is frozen in our subconscious. It's likely to be experiencing the hundreds of fight or flight reactions as well, and reliving them repeatedly. It's holding the trauma so that we don't have to, because we couldn't function efficiently in that state for a prolonged period.

It doesn't matter how long ago the traumatic event took place – whether we were 13 or three, a toddler or 90 years old at the time – the ECHO is stored in the subconscious mind and is reliving the trauma over and over again.

Dr Robert Scaer refers to this process as creating a 'trauma capsule'. In each trauma capsule, everything happening at that moment is recorded: breathing patterns, beliefs, bodily chemical changes, what is being eaten, what is being said, a look that is given… It is all recorded and held within the ECHO.

In Matrix Reimprinting our job is to move the ECHO through the trauma, help them release the freeze response and reduce all the symptoms of fight and flight so that they can move to a place of resourcefulness. We don't see them as being inside us, but outside, in our personal field, our personal Matrix, which, of course, is part of the larger Matrix that connects everything on this Earth.

Why Clear the ECHO's Stress and Trauma?

We tune in to an ECHO when we are triggered by something external that reminds us of the traumatic event in which the ECHO is still stuck. The trigger might be a comment that gets under our skin – perhaps we're called an attention-seeker, or fat, thin, lazy, etc. Whatever it is, it will signal an alert in the subconscious mind, which will then tune us back in to the original ECHO. Suddenly we will be flooded with the energy of the memory, although we may not be conscious of it.

Why does this happen? It appears that our subconscious mind is trying to protect us from the trauma occurring again.

Meet Mo, who wanted to resolve his snake phobia. He couldn't even look at a picture of a snake without breaking into a hot sweat, feeling his throat seizing up and wanting to run away. Just the image of a snake produced a totally irrational fear.

When Karl worked with Mo, the memory that presented itself was of 13-year-old Mo in a bath. A group of older boys had opened the door and thrown a snake into the room and it had landed in his bathwater. The 13-year-old ECHO felt powerless and that there was a threat to his survival, so part of his consciousness split off to hold this trauma. Hence Mo had a 13-year-old ECHO that was frozen and petrified of snakes. This ECHO was part of the filing system in his personal Matrix. Therefore every time Mo saw an image of a snake, or even heard someone speaking about one, it triggered the response that the 13-year-old ECHO was feeling in the Matrix.

This is only the start of Mo's snake story and in Chapter 13 you can read more about how this phobia actually meant something quite different for Mo and underpinned his belief about being abandoned.

It requires a lot of energy to hold information in ECHOs and keep them out of our conscious mind, especially if we have had lots of trauma in our life and get retriggered repeatedly. The number of ECHOs we have and the energy it takes to keep them in place increase over our lifetime and this results in high levels of stress, which we all know can be detrimental to the body.

We often think that our 'issues' will get better with age, but actually they tend to get worse. Our body simply can't take the stress any more. When we're a teenager, our subconscious filing cabinets will already be quite full. By the time we reach adulthood, some files will have reached bursting point and perhaps the cabinet drawer simply can't shut any more and the lock is busted, so it gets harder and harder to keep these traumas out of our mind – and if they're in our mind, then they're in our body.

Why We Need ECHOs

Why create ECHOs in the first place? In essence, we need them. Without them we'd all be walking around in permanent states of trauma. These isolated parts of ourselves are doing a good job holding all that negative energy out of our daily existence. They hold all the information about the trauma so that we don't have to. They're part of our human design.

How Do We Create an ECHO?

The only thing we need to create an ECHO is a threat to survival combined with powerlessness – 'I can't run, I can't fight back' – which is relative to our age and our ability to deal with the situation. For an adult, it may take a significant event to create a new traumatic picture (sudden grief, physical/sexual abuse or an extreme accident). But think of a child, who is small, helpless and has no power over adults. Their survival is constantly being threatened and all it will take to create an ECHO is being told something negative by the people around them (parents, teachers, siblings, caregivers). A child's threshold for trauma and sense of powerlessness are both set much lower than those of adults.

ECHO Personality

ECHOs are energetic realities with real personalities. You may find it a little strange that we're talking about ECHOs as if they were real people. It's true that they don't have a molecular body, but energetically they're just as real as we are.

As soon as we communicate with ECHOs it will become clear that we're working in a different energetic dimension, as they'll give us insights, resources and answers that are often beyond the realm of our conscious awareness.

How Many ECHOs Do We Have?

We have hundreds of both positive and negative ECHOs in our subconscious, filed under various beliefs like 'I'm not good enough' or 'I will be hurt in relationships.' And, as we know, if we're holding these images in our subconscious mind, we'll continue to attract similar events. This will result in a build-up of ECHOs with a certain belief or form of behaviour. We call this an 'ECHO stream'.

A good example of this is when Kate worked with Suzanne, a 37-year-old woman suffering from anxiety, who had felt completely alone in the world since her mother had died 10 years previously.

Together, they visited three separate ECHOs. The first was when Suzanne was 15 and was in a car park smoking. Three older boys came over and one of them sexually assaulted her. Suzanne's ECHO was frozen, felt completely alone and wanted comfort from her mother but felt unable to tell her about the incident because of the smoking.

After working with this teenage ECHO to clear the trauma, they followed the ECHO stream to a memory where Suzanne was nine years old and staying at her grandmother's house. The nine-year-old ECHO didn't want to be there and felt alone. She'd also fallen off a wall and again wanted to be with her mother.

After clearing the energy in this memory, they again followed the ECHO stream, this time back to a six-month-old ECHO who was spending the night alone in hospital after an allergic reaction. They cleared the negative trapped energy and enabled the six-month-old ECHO to feel loved and connected with her family, especially her mother.

This is a brief snapshot of three of Suzanne's ECHOs that had been 'filed' under the same heading in the subconscious, compounding her belief that she was alone in the world and disconnected from her mother, despite having a loving family and having had a 'great' relationship with her mother when she was alive.

It's important to note that each of these memories was visited at least twice during the course of Suzanne's sessions.

Suzanne had kept the ECHOs out of her conscious mind for many years, but when her mother had died it had triggered all of that energy in her subconscious and she had been constantly flooded with it, which had resulted in her anxiety.

The Benefits of Working with ECHOs

Whereas in the EFT Movie Technique we have to keep connecting to the individual aspects of the memory, which can take time and is similar to being drip-fed the emotions, in Matrix Reimprinting we work with an ECHO, the repository of every single bit of information that was stored at that moment, which means that the energy clears quickly as we move the ECHO through the trauma.

In summary, our ECHOs are stuck in the freeze response held in our subconscious mind, our personal Matrix. If we can release this freeze, turn off the fight or flight response and safely move the ECHO through the trauma, we'll reset our current-day response and our bodily systems can let go of the stress.

If the ECHO is no longer in a state of stress, we won't be constantly triggering our HPA axis and releasing stress hormones into our blood owing to misperceptions or incorrect belief systems. We can clear out some of those drawers in the subconscious mind so that it's no longer draining our energy keeping them out of our conscious mind.

Principle 2: Tapping

The main difference between traditional EFT/Tapping and Matrix Reimprinting is that in Matrix Reimprinting we treat ECHOs as younger, separate parts of ourselves with which we can communicate.

We release the trauma from them by tapping on them in the Matrix. It's no more complicated than that.

For example, in EFT, if we had a memory of feeling scared because our parents were shouting at each other, we would use the set-up 'Even though my parents are shouting at each other, I love and accept myself.' In Matrix Reimprinting we would become the EFT practitioner of that five-year-old (the ECHO) and tap on them instead. There's no need for a long set-up because the ECHO is already tuned in to the problem and we use language that is appropriate to their age.

Also, whereas the Movie Technique is like watching a movie of our memory, Matrix Reimprinting is like being in a play. Both techniques start the same way – we tune in to our energy, find a memory and locate the ECHO – but in the Movie Technique we tap on ourselves for everything that the ECHO is feeling and clear all the aspects as they come up, while in Matrix Reimprinting we communicate with the ECHO, they communicate back, and we tap on them and clear their energy very quickly.

Using EFT as part of Matrix Reimprinting may be an advanced concept, but in reality it's easier and quicker to learn and use than standard EFT.

The Set-up
In Matrix Reimprinting there's no need for a long set-up where we repeat the set-up phrase three times. This is because, as noted earlier, the ECHO is already tuned in. They are in the midst of the trauma, so they don't need a long 'hello' to the problem. We also want to get tapping round the points as soon as possible to bring down the intensity of the trauma.

Language
When we speak to an ECHO, the language we use is much more conversational than the formal EFT set-up. The age of the ECHO is

very important here, as we must speak to them in a language they understand. For example, a three-year-old would have problems saying 'I love and accept myself', let alone understanding all that it meant. They would, however, understand 'I'm a good little girl.' So it's important to meet them where they are at. Tap and talk to them in their language. It's a fluid process. It's also a way of creating a sense of community with the ECHO, as often they are feeling alone and that no one is on their side.

Scales of Measurement: SUDS and SUE

In Matrix Reimprinting, the ECHO itself is the SUDS level: we don't need to take a measurement from it. After all, a young ECHO will have trouble numbering their emotional distress and any ECHO will be in the midst of the trauma, so we need to release the energy first. Instead, we take a measurement from ourselves, or our client, before we go into the Matrix. Also, we use the SUE (subjective units of energy) scale (*see page 78*) during the reimprinting part of the process that supercharges our work with the Law of Attraction.

Who Taps When?

In Matrix Reimprinting, we tap on the ECHO. Or, if working with a client, we predominately tap on the client. This is so that the client is free to tap on the ECHO.

How do we tap on ECHOs? Energetically. With clients, think of it as a tapping line into the Matrix: the practitioner will be physically tapping on the client and the client will be energetically tapping on their ECHO in their mind's eye.

As we're only using EFT to reduce the trauma for the ECHO, we don't tap full EFT rounds the whole way through the session, but only when we're releasing the trapped energy that the ECHO is holding. The tapping will release the energetic disturbance and freeze response so that the ECHO can move through it.

Only tapping full rounds to release trauma allows us or our client more time in the Matrix for deep listening and heart-centred questioning. Remember, the ECHO is the real client in this session. Either we are the practitioner (when working on our own ECHOs), or our client becomes the practitioner (when working on their ECHOs), which is immensely healing. Imagine revisiting a part of yourself that needs help and being able to offer it.

If you work with clients via Skype or the telephone, the client will be tapping on themselves as well as on their ECHO. As long as they know the tapping points and feel a sense of community with the ECHO and the practitioner, then face-to-face and virtual sessions work equally powerfully.

Tapping Points

As there's no need for a long set-up statement, we don't need to linger at the karate chop point. The set-up is diluted into the language as we release the trauma. All the facial tapping points are used, yet we don't use the underarm point. This is because it's awkward to tap on this location when we're working with a client. Instead, we use the wrist point, where all the finger meridians meet, tapping firmly across the wrist either side. There is also the option of tapping the wrists together.

As discussed, we only tap full rounds to release trauma, yet at all other times we can tap gently on our finger points, karate chop point and wrist. When we're working with a client, this is especially important, as it builds rapport. Holding the hand of the client and tapping on the finger points puts them at ease and strengthens the bond between us.

Secondary Gains

Another area to be aware of is secondary gains. This is where we or a client have something to lose if we let go of the problem. This can be caused by fear, trauma, historic events, decisions, beliefs, stress and energy toxins, and is common when dealing with depression, addictions and chronic physical ailments. It results in a negative, self-sabotaging state which may appear as resistance and may affect the efficiency of tapping on the main problem.

> Meet Rebecca. She had ME and at one point was bedbound and completely reliant on her family for support. Working with a Matrix Reimprinting practitioner, she was able to make huge strides, but one morning, when she was able to get out of bed, she phoned the practitioner and said that she no longer wanted to continue their work together. She didn't want to get better – she wanted to go back to bed.

> It transpired that because she was no longer bedbound, her son hadn't visited her, her husband had stayed out late and her lunch hadn't been delivered in its usual way. The secondary gain from her illness was receiving the love and attention from her family that she felt that she wouldn't get if she were well.

This is also a reminder that with this work we can only go where clients are willing to take us, and we all have our own journeys to make.

Younger ECHOs don't usually have secondary gains, as they haven't yet developed that strategy, but a client may have issues which are preventing an ECHO from moving forwards. Treat these secondary gains with care and approach them like another belief system to clear, following the stream back to core beliefs.

Gentle Techniques

In EFT there are 'gentle' techniques such as the Tearless Trauma Technique, where the idea is to sneak up on the problem and collapse every aspect of it before it reaches a point of emotional intensity. We also believe it's massively important to keep the client safe, which is why we have a specific step entitled 'Create a Safe Strategy'. Yet the beauty of Matrix Reimprinting as a whole is that it is a very gentle technique.

The aim is to keep ourselves and our clients safely dissociated from the trauma. This also means that people who are already extremely dissociated and find standard EFT difficult, as they can't tune in to how they feel, become especially easy to work with.

Beliefs

As mentioned earlier, Matrix Reimprinting is like participating in a play, being an actor in the theatre of our mind. Not only does it resolve the trauma, it changes the memory and creates supportive fields – it writes a happy ending.

With EFT there is often a void after a situation has been resolved. Matrix Reimprinting fills this void with supportive pictures and positive beliefs. Importantly, it sends a message to the body that the trauma is over, and through the reimprinting process it powerfully invokes the Law of Attraction.

It also quickly finds the belief system. We always ask the ECHO, 'What was the belief or decision that you made that day?' and we bring this information into our conscious mind and can then decide whether it serves us.

We can learn so much from understanding why we've formed our beliefs. We can see how we've built up certain behaviour patterns or why our body has developed a disease. Matrix Reimprinting gives us our belief blueprint and enables us to transform it in a systematic, creative and fluid way.

Principle 3: Our Role as Practitioner

There are three roles within a Matrix Reimprinting session:

1. The practitioner
2. The client
3. The ECHO

The ECHO is of utmost importance. Without it, there is no technique. It also becomes the client, as it is holding all the trauma that needs releasing. When the pictures/memories of the trauma surface, the practitioner guides the client to communicate with the ECHO and release the trauma, create resolution and imprint a new positive picture. Or, when working on themselves, the practitioner communicates with the ECHO directly.

One of the most important parts of working with clients is developing listening skills and 'getting out of the way' of the client and the ECHO doing their work together. Using open questions and clean, clear language, the practitioner simply guides the client to work with the ECHO so that they can gain realizations for themselves.

Leading on from this, our main role as practitioner is to explain the process and offer suggestions if and when the client gets stuck. It is important that the ideas for resources, safe locations, reframes, changing the outcome, etc., come from the client and their ECHOs.

It is also a practitioner's role to steer the client or ECHO away from making inappropriate choices.

We'd like to add a note here about the ethics of changing subconscious memories. We are not denying that the trauma happened. Neither are we changing the course of history. Matrix Reimprinting is simply removing the energy of the trauma that is held in the subconscious and changing the perception and the negative beliefs that have resulted from it. It would be wrong to deny that traumatic events happened. But with Matrix Reimprinting we can release the trauma and move on from it.

Principle 4: The Role of the Heart

The heart has a massively important role in how we communicate energetically with the world. It's a powerful electromagnetic transmitter which radiates an energetic pulse three metres (10 feet) from our body in a 360-degree sphere, broadcasting information 24 hours a day. It is 60 times electrically and 5,000 times magnetically more powerful than the brain.

The Institute of HeartMath in California has been doing scientific research into the role of the heart for over two decades and has found that there is 'a nervous system pathway that carries signals from the heart to the brain, as well as one that carries messages from the brain to the heart. Surprisingly, the heart sends more signals to the brain that the brain sends to the heart.'[1]

What information is the heart sending to the brain? We believe that it's the information that is stored in the subconscious field. The heart is the transmitter to and from the Matrix. In Matrix Reimprinting we use the heart consciously to send out the new supportive pictures as part of the reimprinting process, thus making our work in the field even more powerful.

When we bring collective consciousness into the equation and factor in how our heart fields can influence each other, it opens up another dialogue about how changing our personal fields can affect the human race as a whole. The Institute of HeartMath's study showed that 'when two people are at a conversational distance, the electromagnetic signal generated by one person's heart can influence the other person's brain rhythms'.[2] This research is exciting and scientifically ground-breaking, and yet part of us already knows that we are all connected and we affect one another on both a conscious and a subconscious level. As we move through the chapters in this book towards creating a life of holistic happiness, you'll learn even more about how important our own healing and vibrational alignment are for the rest of the human race.

We also use 'heart breathing' in Matrix Reimprinting. Focusing the breath through the heart isn't a new concept. Buddhists have been using it in meditation for hundreds of years and the Institute of

HeartMath has developed fantastic coherence techniques that you can learn more about by visiting its content-rich website.[3]

We've found heart breathing a fantastic tool, first for ensuring that both client and practitioner are consciously present at the beginning of a session and second for grounding a client if they become associated with the ECHO and experience a high level of distress. Focused heart breathing is an easy way to instantly bring a person back to their centre. Would you like to try it?

Using Heart Breathing

1. Close your eyes and relax into your chair.

2. Put your hand over your heart and focus your attention into that area, into those deep chambers in the centre of your chest.

3. Breathe deeply but normally and feel as if your breath is coming in and out of your heart area.

4. Begin to regulate your breathing to a count of six.

5. Breathe for a count of six seconds into your heart space.

6. Breathe for a count of six seconds out of your heart space.

7. Keep breathing in for six and breathing out for six.

8. Focus on your heart area and feel the relaxation.

Notice how relaxed you feel. It's easy yet powerful and perfect for clients who are experiencing any level of distress.

◆◆◆◆◆

Once you've grasped these four principles, you have the foundations of Matrix Reimprinting. It's now time to learn the seven simple steps of the Classic Matrix Reimprinting Technique. Here you'll be able to put all you've learned into practice and begin to change the information in your fields, explore your core beliefs and, importantly, discover how they've affected your life so far – not forgetting how you'd like them to influence your life in the future.

Chapter 6

THE CLASSIC MATRIX
REIMPRINTING TECHNIQUE

Picture yourself winning the Wimbledon tennis trophy, standing there in front of a cheering crowd... Seems impossible, right? But although the winner of that trophy has to put in hours of training to hit a tennis ball at amazing speed, it will only take a bit of coaching and a few hours of practice to hit a volley and be good enough to play a game of tennis.

Becoming a Matrix Reimprinting practitioner won't take a lifetime of tapping practice in all weathers, but it will require becoming proficient in the Classic Technique. Then, once you know the basic steps, you can adapt them for the different life themes and client issues with which you want to work.

The Classic Matrix Reimprinting Steps

1. Find the ECHO.
2. Create a safe strategy.
3. Tap to release the freeze.
4. ECHO Check-in.
5. ECHO Belief resolution.
6. Reimprinting process.
7. Measuring success.

There are seven steps, but essentially these three illustrations cover the process beautifully:

Recalling the memory: You have a memory, for example of your parents arguing when you were a child.

Using EFT with the ECHO: You step into the memory and tap on the ECHO.

Resolution and reimprinting: Find resolution and end with a positive picture to reimprint.

Step 1: Find the ECHO

✧ Close your eyes and see in your mind's eye the memory that you wish to work on.

Everyone has a different way of seeing themselves or having a sense of themselves. Be aware of how you 'see' your younger self, the ECHO (auditory/visual/kinaesthetic).

If you are working with a client, check in with them about how they 'see' their ECHO. This will give you a steer on the language to use. It is also advisable to ask them if it's OK for you to tap on them.

Step 2: Create a Safe Strategy

✧ In a moment you're going to step into that picture and talk to the ECHO. Your aim is to tap on them as soon as possible to release the pain and trauma they're feeling. How can you make the process safe for them? Do you need to stop everything and everyone else in the picture before you go in and tap on them? If, for example, there's an ECHO who is being bullied, do you need to block the perpetrator off? Freeze them? Put a wall in front of them? Gag them? In extreme cases, you can suggest that the ECHO goes to a safe place and then work with them there before going back into the original memory.

When working with a client, it's important that they know it's a joint effort between the two of you to help the ECHO. Keep the memory to one side while you decide on the safe strategy that you will use as a team.

It is of utmost importance to stay dissociated from the ECHO, as this will keep you and the client safe and won't trigger all the negative emotion or energy that they're feeling.

To ensure a client stays dissociated, you can ask a number of questions such as 'What is your younger self wearing?' or 'What do they look like?' Gently remind them to look at their younger self and to treat them as a person and remain separate from them.

There are two ways in which you may become associated. The first is that the energy of the ECHO enters you so that you tune in to what they are feeling. This is the way that standard EFT is taught, so you feel every single aspect that comes up and use EFT to reduce the distress. Most of the time this is fine, but it also means that you take on all the trauma in the body and this can in some cases cause severe abreactions. One of the benefits of Matrix Reimprinting is that it avoids abreactions by keeping you separate from the trauma.

The second way you may become associated is that you step into being the ECHO. This is likely to happen if there's no safety strategy in place. You simply open the door to that memory and bang, suddenly become that younger self again, feeling all the trauma you felt the first time you experienced the situation. To avoid this, have a clear safety strategy in place first.

You'll know if a client has become associated with the ECHO as they will feel all the trauma that their ECHO is holding and will show signs of distress. Ask them if they've become the ECHO and ask them to step out of the ECHO and to see their ECHO as a separate being. Often this will be enough to change the state.

If they can't do that, ask them to come out of the memory and go in again slowly, keeping themselves distant from the ECHO. If they're especially triggered, use the heart breathing technique. Never be afraid to suggest a new safe strategy for the client, using gentle techniques and insightful questioning.

Step 3: Tap to Release the Freeze

✧ Step into the picture and ask the ECHO how they are feeling.

✧ Tap on them to release the energy/freeze response.

It's important to get tapping as soon as possible to release the freeze response and clear the trauma that the ECHO has been holding. Remember there's no need to do a complicated set-up because they're already tuned in. This is a fluid conversation rather than a rigid protocol – you'll say something different each time. All you need to remember is where the tapping points are.

When working with a client, ask them to talk to the ECHO and find out what emotion they are feeling and where they are feeling it in their body. Then the client taps on the ECHO while you tap around the points on the client, repeating reminder phrases and reducing the energy.

For example, if the ECHO is feeling a yellow ball of fear in their stomach, you'll start on the client's karate chop point while they imagine tapping on their ECHO's karate chop point. At the same time, you'll be repeating the description of the energy out loud, with your client repeating it after you; for example: 'This yellow ball of fear in your heart... all of this fear.' Adapt the language to the age of the ECHO and, as in regular EFT, continue tapping until the emotion has reduced or changed, listening out for those cognitive shifts.

Also add in phrases to help the ECHO feel safe and give them a sense of community:

✧ 'It's over.'

✧ 'You're safe.'

✧ 'I'm here to help.'

✧ 'You're not alone.'

Step 4: ECHO Check-in

Our first job is to release the ECHO's trauma. Our second job is to find the belief and decisions that the ECHO made that day and help them create the opposite of that belief using the resources available.

✧ Ask the ECHO how they are feeling and check that all the energy/freeze response has been released. Continue tapping until all the trauma held by the ECHO has been cleared.

✧ Ask, 'What belief or decision did you make about yourself that day? What did you learn about life that day?'

When working with a client, after one or two rounds of EFT encourage the client to talk to the ECHO about how they are feeling. Has the energy subsided? Has it changed or moved to somewhere else in their body?

It's important that the client listens to the ECHO and takes note of what they're upset about. It might be that the ECHO says, 'Mummy doesn't love me.' This is an opportunity to explore this and gently guide the ECHO to a place where they believe they are loved.

Step 5: ECHO Belief Resolution

✧ What resources does the ECHO need to create resolution? Do they need to bring another family member in? A favourite toy or pet? They might want to go somewhere else. For example, in a memory where an ECHO has been abused, you can't create a 'nice' picture, so the ECHO will understandably want to go somewhere else. It's not black and white – actually, it's a rainbow of possibilities. But it's a very easy process as long as we hold the space and allow all the possibilities for resolution to come directly from the ECHO.

If you're working with a client, remind them that it is a joint endeavour to help the ECHO feel better and create a harmonious situation. You can make suggestions, but, as with all change work, the resources need to come from the ECHO and the client themselves, and this is where open questioning, clear language and listening skills come into their own. Often this work is done in silence. Give the client the time they need.

When you're changing the picture, remember to keep it directly relevant to the belief or decision that was formed and only bring in other people – parents, friends, etc. – if that's what's needed. For example, if a four-year-old ECHO felt scared and not good enough after being reprimanded by her mother, ask her if she would like to bring in her mother and speak to her about how she felt. Encourage the mother to talk to the ECHO and tell her she is safe and loved, and how sorry she is for shouting.

We can presume that mothers are likely to empathize with their children. But what about an attacker or someone who has abused the ECHO? This is where the concept of the 'higher self' is important. The higher self is an elevated consciousness of a person. In the Matrix it is often the higher selves who come in to speak to the ECHOs. This helps us to realize that no one is 100 per cent good or 100 per cent evil; we're all products of the events we've lived through. For example, it's likely that an abuser will themselves have been abused in the past. By asking their higher self to come in, you're creating a safe strategy and also a place for healing and forgiveness.

Previously in Matrix Reimprinting we often over-resourced our clients by always inviting other people in (the Dalai Lama, John Lennon, pop stars, etc.), or magical resources (magic carpets, fairy wands), and also asking the ECHOs if they would like to go somewhere else (beach, forest). Many clients may not have even needed these resources. In truth, all the answers were inside them anyway. Also, what message are we giving our ECHOs if they always need someone else's help to resolve an issue? That they can't do it on their own? We want the ECHOs to feel empowered and independent. Keeping the change as close to the original memory as possible also ensures that there is only one picture in the Matrix rather than two.

The SUE Scale

Once the ECHO has achieved resolution, it's time to build up this positive picture using all the senses. Whereas we used the SUDS scale previously, we now use the SUE (subjective units of energy) scale, which goes from −10 to +10:

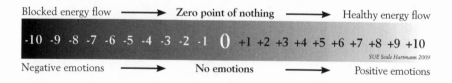

The SUE scale

The SUE scale was developed by Silvia Hartmann, a pioneer in Energy Psychology techniques.[1] It's a fantastic tool, as it highlights what else might need releasing in the memory. There may be something that's not quite right or the resolution could be made stronger by talking to another family member. It may transpire that the family member also needs some tapping and releasing before they're able to communicate in a heartfelt way.

(For more about bringing in other people and surrogate tapping, see Chapter 7.)

Our aim is to get this picture to a +10 for the ECHO. If it's about a +8 picture, what would make it a +10? Again, it's important that most of the suggestions come from the ECHO themselves.

Step 6: Reimprinting Process

You (or your client) will now have a powerful picture in your mind's eye, ideally rating high on the SUE scale. You may also have an idea of the belief that has stemmed from the memory.

Now it is time for the reimprint. This is a personal process and everyone will do it differently. It's best to take your time, as it's here that the new belief and emotions are sent to all the cells in the body and also out into the universe.

You have complete creative licence with this process. Below is the most technical way of reimprinting, but the most important part to remember is to send the picture to all the cells and also utilize the body's most powerful transmitter, the heart.

✧ Take in (or ask the client to take in) the following information in the picture:
- all the feelings and positive emotions of the ECHO, especially the feeling of community

- all associated sounds, smells, (bodily) sensations, etc.

- the positive belief/decision that the ECHO associates with this new memory (the opposite of the negative belief/decision in the original memory)

- the colours appearing around the picture

- ✧ When this is as vivid as possible, bring the picture towards you and pull it, complete with all the sensory information, into your head and send it through your entire brain, through all of the cells and the neural pathways.

- ✧ Now send this information through the rest of your body whilst focusing on (if applicable):
  - organs or body parts which are ill or hurt

  - organs or body parts which are involved in the old behavioural pattern

  - body parts which are in some way affected by the emotional issue

- ✧ Imagine all your cells attuning to and aligning with this new information until your body has totally absorbed it.

- ✧ Then put one hand on your heart and take all the information of the new picture into your heart. Take some time to deepen the new belief in your heart. Intensify all feelings, emotions, sensations and other positive impressions, and make the associated colours even brighter.

- ✧ Send this picture out from your heart in all directions, so that you become a beacon sending light back into the Matrix, back into the whole universe, into all the dimensions of time and space, into all the dimensions of your being – into everywhere imaginable.

Step 7: Measuring Success

After the reimprinting process, it's time to check in with the original memory.

- ✧ Close your eyes (or ask your client to close their eyes) and tune back into the original memory.

- ✧ What has changed? What work is left to do?

We *always* go into every memory at least twice, and often many more times, to find the deeper lessons hidden within it. If the ECHO is still a little bit sad or perhaps a parent doesn't look happy, this shows that there's more work to be done. It's just another layer that's come up, that's all. It will also give you a starting point for the next session.

Moving through the Steps

Below is an example of a 10-minute client session where the practitioner moved through the steps quickly and easily:

Practitioner: Can you see yourself in this picture?

Client: *Yes, I'm in the front room at home.*

Practitioner: How old are you and what are you wearing?

Client: *I'm about nine and I think I'm wearing a white dress.*

Practitioner: We are going to work together as a team and go in and help your nine-year-old self. You're going to do some tapping with her and it's important that you remain separate and listen to what she has to say. Is that OK?

Client: *Yes.*

Practitioner: Do we need to freeze anyone in the picture?

Client: *No, she's there on her own.*

Practitioner: Step into the picture, introduce yourself to her and explain that you're there to help her feel better and you're going to do some tapping with her. Let me know if you need help or when you've finished.

Client: *OK. She's feeling scared.*

Practitioner: Ask her where that scared feeling is in her body.

Client: *It's in her stomach.*

Practitioner: What colour is it and what's she scared of?

Client: *She's scared of her mum's boyfriend and it's a yellow fear in her tummy.*

Practitioner: Take her hand, tap on her where I'm tapping on you and repeat these words out loud after me:

[Karate chop] All this yellow fear in your tummy and you're scared of Mum's boyfriend. You're a good girl, you've done nothing wrong. I love you very much.

[Top of the head] All this yellow fear in your stomach.

[Eyebrow] Scared of Mum's boyfriend.

[Side of the eye] All this yellow fear in your tummy.

[Under eye] So scared of Mum's boyfriend.

[Under nose] All this yellow fear in your tummy.

[Chin] I'm here to help you. You're a good girl.

[Collarbone] This remaining yellow fear in your tummy.

[Wrist] You're safe.

[Thumb] Any remaining fear in your tummy.

[Index finger] Remaining yellow fear in your tummy.

[Middle finger] I'm here to help.

[Ring finger] You're safe to let it go.

[Little finger] You're safe, I'm here.

Practitioner: Ask your nine-year-old self if she's still scared and if that yellow feeling is still there.

Client: *She's feeling better, but is still a bit scared.*

Practitioner: What's she scared of specifically?

Client: *He always shouts at her for not clearing up after dinner, but she just wants to go upstairs and listen to her music.*

Practitioner: I'm going to make a few suggestions and you see which ones feel right to pass on to your younger self. Would she like to talk to her mum's boyfriend about how she's feeling? Does she want to bring Mum in?

Client: *Yes, she wants to talk to Mum.*

Practitioner: OK. Remember that our strategy is to help the younger you feel better. When you feel ready, bring Mum in.

Client: *Mum looks a little bit angry.*

Practitioner: Is Mum OK for us to tap on her?

Client: *Yes, she is.*

Practitioner: Ask Mum where all that anger is in her body. What's the emotion, colour and texture?

Client: *Red anger in her throat.*

Practitioner: Take Mum's hand and tap around the points, repeating, 'All this red anger in your throat.'

Client: *[After a few minutes doing this in silence] Mum isn't angry any more. She's feeling guilty.*

Practitioner: OK, where does she feel that guilt?

Client: *It's in her stomach. She feels guilty for not being there and having to work late.*

Practitioner: Take Mum's hand and tap around her points, saying, 'All this guilt in your tummy, feeling so guilty about having to work late and not being there after school. You're a good mum, you're doing the best you can. All of this guilt in your tummy, you're doing a good job.'

Practitioner: Ask Mum why she has to work late.

Client: *She has to work hard so that she can pay the bills and take her on holiday. She loves her so much. [Sobs]*

Practitioner: It's OK.

Client: *[After a few moments] I feel better now. I'm going to talk to Mum.*

Practitioner: I'll be quiet. Let me know if you need help or when it feels complete.

Client: *OK... she's talked to Mum about how she feels and Mum's giving her a big hug.*

Practitioner: Great. Ask her if she's still feeling scared.

Client: *A bit scared that her mum's boyfriend might still shout at her.*

Practitioner: Could she speak to Mum about that and see if Mum has any ideas?

Client: *OK... Mum says she'll speak to Rob [boyfriend].*

Practitioner: I'm going to be quiet and let Mum and you speak to Rob about how the little you is feeling. Let me know when that feels complete.

[A few minutes elapse...]

Client: *Rob is saying sorry and that I can listen to my music. Mum is smiling and Rob is smiling too.*

Practitioner: Is she still scared?

Client: *No.*

Practitioner: Ask her what she believed about herself and the world that day.

Client: *That she always got told off for not clearing up! That's probably why I get so het up about the washing-up now and nag my children. It's true, I do find it hard to relax and have fun. I feel that I always have to be doing something, whether that's cleaning the house or working on a project. I'm not really allowed to have fun – I always have to work. It makes such sense to me now. I've been running this my whole life! I can even see myself at university – when all my friends were going out, I was studying or bloody cleaning!*

Practitioner: OK, you're going to create a harmonious situation for the younger you now where she feels that she can relax. Ask her what she would like to do right now.

Client: *She just wants to sit and listen to her music and feel safe in her bedroom.*

Practitioner: Great. What music is it?

Client: *New Kids on the Block. [Laughs]*

Practitioner: Ask her how happy she feels out of 10 right now.

Client: *About an eight.*

Practitioner: What would make it a 10?

Client: *She'd like Mum there and Rob smiling at her. Plus sunshine coming through the window.*

Practitioner: Great. Make this picture as vivid as possible. Turn up all the colours, emotions and brightness. What are the colours?

Client: *There's a pink glow around it and I can see red poppies on her bedspread.*

Practitioner: Really feel that positivity and that gorgeous pink glow. Bring that picture towards you and pull it down into your head, into every cell, every interconnection. Then move that beautiful picture down your body. Imagine all your cells are now attuning to this lovely feeling of being relaxed. Wash it over your shoulders, your body, your legs, so that you're vibrating this gorgeous pink glow. When you feel ready, place one hand on your heart and bring that picture up into your heart. Really see that younger you enjoying her music, relaxing with Mum and Rob smiling at her. See that lovely pink energy and the red poppies on the bedspread. Know it's OK to relax. Make that pink even brighter. Then, when you're ready, send that picture out from your heart into the universe and beyond.

Client: *Ah, that was lovely.*

Practitioner: Have some water and then tune back in to that original picture. What's your nine-year-old self doing in the bedroom?

Client: *She's lying back on her bedspread with her headphones on, listening to the music.*

Practitioner: Ask her if she's feeling OK and whether she has any other worries we can help her with.

Client: *She's enjoying her music, but she's missing Mum, who has to work every day and is never there when she comes home from school, and her dad never calls her either.*

Practitioner: Thank her for this information and let her know that you'll come back and help her with these issues at a later date.

As you can see from this snapshot, which was only a 10-minute session, the Classic Technique is easy to learn. If you want to become proficient in it, it won't take long. We estimate about 10 sessions, either on yourself or with a willing recipient, will be enough to learn these simple steps. However, if you'd like to work with paying clients and wish to be insured, you'll need to be experienced in EFT, attend a Matrix Reimprinting training course and complete video training and a test to be awarded practitioner status. Full details can be found in the Resources for Practitioners section at the back of the book (*see page 263*).

Are you ready to move on to Enhanced Matrix Reimprinting? The techniques you'll learn will complement the Classic steps and soon you'll be able to take a trip down an ECHO stream, systematically change morphic fields and enhance your work in the Matrix.

Chapter 7

ENHANCED MATRIX REIMPRINTING

Matrix Reimprinting is truly about deep work. It allows you to explore the lessons, perceptions and beliefs that underpin your life through the traumas you've experienced. Anyone can learn the four principles and apply the Classic Technique, but it takes commitment, confidence and flexibility to enhance your work in the Matrix.

Why Enhance It?

As you've probably guessed by now, it's that seven-letter word again: beliefs. It's through our core beliefs that we shape our physiology and our life. If we can trace them back through ECHO streams and imprint positive pictures, we'll create supportive beliefs instead.

Discovering Some of Your Beliefs

1. Tune in to your inner landscape.

2. Close your eyes.

3. Take a breath.

   - Do you believe you're good enough to get your dream job?

   - What about finding (and keeping) your ideal partner?

– Are you good enough to have a family?

– Are you a good enough parent?

◆◆◆◆◆

Having this 'not good enough' belief is epidemic in our society. Most of us resonate with it on some level and many of us let it get out of control, never believing we're 'quite good enough' to live the life we want to.

Would you like that to change? Where did it come from, anyway? Why do you believe you aren't good enough? What would your life look like if you took the right opportunities, no matter if they were big and scary? What if, in your soul, you knew you were good enough to take them?

This is why we start with the Classic Matrix Technique and encourage people to use it on any memory that presents itself. Within each memory there will be a belief. It might not be apparent the first few times you go into the Matrix, but with practice, beliefs show up like puddles after the rain has stopped. What then?

Revisiting Memories

Karl has a motto about going into memories at least twice. It's not a failing to go into a memory again – the failing is not going back in. There is such emotional depth to each memory that it takes several revisits to understand the precise belief. Often, more than one belief comes from one memory.

> *Kate was working with a client called Kelly on a memory of her childhood. She was nine years old and feeling traumatized because her mother had come in drunk, had fallen and cut her head open and had reached out to her while her father had been on the phone to the ambulance.*
>
> *The first time they worked with the ECHO, they cleared young Kelly's confusion about what was happening and the fact that she felt so unsafe in the world and around her unpredictable mother in particular.*

The trauma was released and a new picture imprinted. Yet Kate knew there was more to do in this memory, as it was such a powerful one for Kelly, whose entire childhood had been spent at the mercy of her unpredictable mother.

In the next session, they revisited the scene. Because so much of the flight, fight, freeze trauma had already been released in the first session, the ECHO could now access other depths about what happened that day. They found that she had felt completely overwhelmed when her mother had reached out to her, but hadn't known how to tell her father how scared she felt and had decided she 'had to put a brave face on and hide it'.

Kelly's core belief was that if she ever felt scared she had to put a brave face on it and hide it. This resulted in hyper-vigilance and low energy levels in her current reality.

This was a turning point in their sessions together and Kelly's energy levels moved up significantly from then on.

It could be that we revisit a memory straight away, potentially when we're measuring for success or at the start of the next session. Either way, we'll find that the picture has changed and the ECHO has new meanings for us. Even when the SUDS level is zero, if we go back in we'll find profound new meanings and beliefs.

We can also test the 'Validity of Cognition' of beliefs by simply saying the belief out loud, tuning in to how it feels and giving a percentage of how true it feels. This can show us how our beliefs have collapsed over the time we've been working on them.

Finding the Earliest ECHO

We want to find the earliest ECHO in the ECHO stream, as the further back we go, the more likely we are to find the core event, the one that will reduce the energy in the stream afterwards.

For example, if we want to stem the flow of 'I'm not good enough' in our life, there will be many ECHOs swimming in this stream. However, there will be a core event that started this stream – one that arose as a spring and subsequently leaked out into the fields, creating puddles, pools and eventually fast-flowing streams. If we trace the stream back through the fields, mopping up the water as we go, we'll finally reach that spring.

A mountain spring is a beautiful image, but we may feel that our core events aren't glorious at all. Nevertheless, as we work with these traumas, we'll eventually see that they have a purpose, that they're part of our journey to clear ancestral patterns and that they help us open ourselves up spiritually. It is then that we'll be grateful for them and see them as events to be cherished.

Memories that generate core beliefs are often unconscious or blocked. There are three techniques that we use in Matrix Reimprinting to find them: Following the Energy, Slow EFT and ECHO to ECHO. We can also use a combination of all three.

Following the Energy

When we tap, it becomes very apparent that the energy we feel when we tune into a memory is the same energy that we experienced at the time of the original trauma. So we use this technique to tune in to that energy and follow it down the ECHO stream to the causative events themselves.

1. Think of (or ask your client to think of) a specific issue that you'd like to work on. This could be anything, from problems with relationships, money or work to phobias, depression and anxiety, etc.

2. Close your eyes.

3. Take deep breaths, focusing on breathing in and out of your heart and clearing your mind (as you want the information to come from the subconscious and not the conscious mind).

4. Start to tap through the points slowly and gently.

5. State (out loud) the issue you're trying to resolve, e.g., 'I'm anxious about my wife leaving me.'

6. Tune in to the feeling (the tapping will help you do this).

7. Where in the body do you feel this?

8. Say where you feel it while continuing to tap slowly though all the points, e.g., 'This feeling in my stomach...'

9. Describe this feeling?

10. Add this new information to your statement, e.g., 'This big heavy ball in my stomach...'

11. Repeat the above steps, each time adding new information, including size, colour and emotion. Your final words may be something like 'This big red angry feeling in my stomach...'

12. When you have all the information (this usually takes around two to three minutes) and are strongly tuned in to your feelings, ask yourself, 'When was the first time I experienced these feelings?'

If you don't know, guess, as this will bypass the conscious mind. If you're still struggling, think about how old you were and where you might have been. Once the conscious mind is out of the way and you allow this subconscious information to emerge, you'll eventually come up with a memory, often of an event before the age of six, that is the origin of the current problem. If you come up with a memory from later on in life, say at 18, ask yourself, 'If there was an earlier time when I felt this way, when was it?'

At this point we're using the information *just* to access a specific memory. We can then go on to release the trauma and imprint with the Classic Matrix Technique. We can stop at any memory and do some work with the Classic Technique, then go to an earlier memory later if we choose, using the ECHO to ECHO technique (*see page 93*).

◆ ◆ ◆ ◆ ◆

Slow EFT

This technique was developed by Silvia Hartmann, the respected author of many EFT books. Despite being called 'slow', it's actually a fast tool to find a memory or ECHO related to a specific issue and belief. Karl has adapted it for the purposes of Matrix Reimprinting using only three points: the top of the head, collarbone and wrist.

1. Tap on the top of your head as you focus on breathing into your heart chamber. This should be done in a considered way, breathing in for a count of six seconds and out for a count of six seconds.

2. Whilst you're breathing consciously in this way, also use a reminder phrase, for example 'Rejection' or 'I'm not good enough.' (If you're working with clients, this is especially good for working with groups with similar themes.) The reminder phrase should be repeated several times throughout the process and the tapping should be slow and soft.

3. Take time to search through your subconscious field and see and feel what comes up.

4. If nothing comes up whilst tapping on that first point, move on to the collarbone point and repeat the process.

5. Finally, move to the wrist point and change the reminder phrase if needed.

6. Once a relevant thought or memory arises, this is the starting point for working with an ECHO.

◆ ◆ ◆ ◆ ◆

ECHO to ECHO

This technique elegantly leads you back to core events. The premise is simple: once you've worked with an ECHO using the Classic Technique, that 'happy' ECHO takes you down the ECHO stream to an earlier event.

1. Either go to a specific memory or use the 'Following the Energy' technique to locate a relevant memory.

2. Use the Classic Matrix Reimprinting process to work with that ECHO.

3. When the ECHO is no longer traumatized, the negative belief made at the time has been identified and the ECHO has been resourced to create a positive memory, reimprint as normal.

4. Let the ECHO know they can stay in this memory. What you're about to ask them can be daunting for them, so reassure them that they can stay where they are if they wish.

5. Say to them, 'If there had been another time when you needed help, when would that have been?' You can also ask the age or if they will just show you the memory.

6. Often the ECHO will spontaneously take you to another memory without even being asked. They may do so even before you've finished doing all the work on the current memory. If this happens, go with the flow. Resolving other memories has an effect on the memory you're working on, especially when the ECHO jumps to earlier memories. You can always return to the original memory to check what else needs to be done.

◆◆◆◆◆

Meet Julie, who had an issue with rejection and a belief that people would leave her. She accessed a memory of when she was a six-year-old ECHO lost at the seaside. When she stepped in and worked with her younger self, initially that younger self was very scared that Mum and Dad wouldn't find her, so Julie tapped on her to resolve the trauma.

After calming her down, she came out of the memory and explained that little Julie was calm now, but looked really sad.

She stepped back into the memory and asked her younger self why she was so sad. The ECHO told her, 'Mum and Dad don't love me. They lost me on purpose.' When Julie asked, 'Why do you think that?' she instantly took her back to when she was three years old and her parents were shouting at her.

Having done a little work on this memory, resulting in her parents explaining to the three-year-old how much they loved her and giving her a hug, Julie returned to the lost six-year-old on the beach, who was now sitting on a bench smiling. She said, 'I know they love me now. I'll just stay here and look at the sea until they come and find me.'

We often find that working on one event in an ECHO stream has an effect on connected events, and it's always the belief that connects them.

Clearing the Past to Clear the Present

Sometimes it can be difficult to clear a more recent memory, due to a series of similar events over the course of a person's life. In these cases, earlier situations will need to be resolved first. Here are a couple of examples of how working with one ECHO can have dramatic effects on other ECHOs in that belief stream.

Meet Brenda, who wanted to work on her traumatic break-up with her long-term partner earlier that year but kept being told by her ECHO to 'get lost'. All of her attempts to help her ECHO of a few months earlier were met with resistance, rejection and anger.

When Brenda was asked 'When did this issue of rejection start?' she instantly went to a memory of rejection as a five-year-old. It was decided that both the current Brenda and her ECHO of a few months earlier would go back to help the young girl.

Having spent time making the five-year-old feel special, accepted and heard, Brenda returned to the memory of a few months before. The older ECHO now understood her core issue and belief around rejection and was willing to work with her to resolve the painful feelings of the break-up with her partner.

◆◆◆◆◆

Meet Johan, who suffered from PTSD due to his time in the military, where he'd been involved in a number of conflicts in various regions of the world. One of his traumatic memories involved a reconnaissance mission to a crash site containing the burned bodies of dead soldiers.

On the first visit to this memory, Johan's ECHO insisted he was OK and wasn't traumatized by the event. Speaking to the current Johan, who knew this event was one of those behind his PTSD symptoms, he realized, however, that he wasn't allowed to show his emotions. This belief went back to a four-year-old ECHO who was being scolded by his father, who had physically abused him when he'd cried. He had concluded that it wasn't safe to show his emotions and that he had to be perfect to receive his dad's love.

Having worked with both the four-year-old ECHO and his father to get resolution on these beliefs, Johan returned to the crash-site memory. The soldier ECHO was now able to express, and clear, the emotion he felt witnessing this horrendous event.

Combining Echo to Echo and Following the Energy – Nuances

Combining the above techniques can enable us to go back to core issues quickly. The questions we ask the ECHOs will have an effect on how far back the memories go. If we say, 'Remember an earlier time when you felt the same way?' we may just go back to quite recent events, whereas if we ask, 'When was the first time you remember feeling this way?' we will often go back to much earlier events, which are more likely to be the core issues.

There is both an upside and a downside to getting back to the core issue very quickly. On the upside, sooner or later we need to get back to the origin of the problem to clear it fully. However, as we need to elicit the belief formed during these events, if we go back too quickly we may end up working with very young ECHOs who can't express the belief in words.

We've found that a good balance is to start with recent memories and go back step by step to several memories covering a large portion of the person's life to ascertain what the belief is that connects all the memories in the ECHO stream.

If, however, the intention of using the ECHO to ECHO technique is only to find a specific belief, we can just do minimal work and touch in on each memory without doing the full Classic Technique of trauma resolution, resourcing, reimprinting, etc.

Once the specific belief is clear, we can always revisit the memories we touched upon and use the full Classic Technique on each of them.

Although we've described Matrix Reimprinting in steps for the ease of teaching, it's actually a fluid process and every single session is different. No practitioner should be sitting there with a notebook and a manual of the steps to follow – at least not after the first session! It's about listening to the ECHO and finding, or guiding our client to find, our own resolutions and realizations and ultimately facilitate our own healing.

Surrogate Tapping: Tapping on Other People's ECHOs

What should we do if an ECHO wants us to tap on someone else in the memory? What are the ethics of tapping on other people's ECHOs?

The aim of a Matrix session isn't to tap on everyone in the picture, but that's often the wish expressed by the ECHO or client, therefore the right thing to do. It also helps shift other people's ECHOs to a place where they can communicate clearly with the central ECHO and therefore create resolution.

We also know from the thousands of sessions that it can only benefit that person's life. We're doing them a good deed by tapping on them. The question should really be: 'Why wouldn't we do it?'

The option of surrogate tapping is therefore always included (if appropriate) when resourcing the ECHO. Matrix Reimprinting has amazing effects when working surrogately with others, as we are all connected by the Matrix. When we work in the Matrix with other people, the effects ripple out into their reality as well as our own. This means that when we resolve our own issues, the people who were involved in our memories also receive the benefits of our clearing work.

Meet Amber, who had a fear of public speaking. Using the Following the Energy technique, she quickly went back to a six-year-old ECHO who'd been humiliated by her teacher for speaking out in front of her classmates. When the trauma had been cleared, the ECHO wanted to know why the teacher had shouted, as she felt she hadn't done anything wrong.

They talked to the teacher, who was feeling sad and frustrated. He didn't want to shout at the children, but he was tired, as his wife had just had a baby, and he didn't like his boss, the head teacher. They tapped on him, helping him to release all of his tiredness and frustration, and he emerged feeling much happier. Together they imprinted a lovely memory of Amber singing to her classmates.

Belief Brainstorm

Once you've found a core issue or belief, it's important to make a note of it. We recommend using a simple brainstorm (*see below*) to keep track of your beliefs, memories and realizations. You'll also experience deeper, faster change if you concentrate on one life theme or belief at a time.

Whilst we avoid writing notes during a session, we do encourage note-taking after spending time in the Matrix. The more detail you find out about your beliefs and how they're connected to your life events, the easier it is to change them.

In fact, many people (Karl included) receive a huge amount of clarification and healing simply from the realizations themselves. When you realize, as a result of this deep work, where and how your life has been dictated by these beliefs, it reduces the energetic charge around them and you're able to perceive solutions.

How to Create a Belief Brainstorm

1. Grab a blank piece of paper and write your issue or belief in the centre.

2. Give it a VoC rating (a percentage) of how true it is for you right now.

3. List all the memories relating to that theme, radiating out from it in a mind map.

4. Work on them one at a time.

5. When you've changed a memory, you can write the new memory on your mind map if you want to.

◆ ◆ ◆ ◆ ◆

Positive Belief Imprinting

Once you've brainstormed a belief and done enough work on it to reduce the validity, it's time to use Positive Belief Imprinting, which is a systematic way of changing your morphic field and point of attraction. This is achieved by taking the original ECHO to a future ECHO where the issue has been overcome and a new picture of success has been created.

Depending on the strength of the issue, belief and morphic field, a lot of work may be needed to collapse the old fields before you're ready to take the next step with a future ECHO.

This technique works well, however, because when we work with ECHOs we're working in a quantum field where past, present, future and all possibilities exist simultaneously.

Positive Belief Reimprinting

Positive Belief Reimprinting is about tuning in to the morphic field of a positive future reality and then creating a new morphic field around this potentiality in the present.

1. Start with the presenting issue – negative belief, relationship problem, money worry, phobia, depression, anxiety, illness, etc. – and use the recall techniques to get back to a specific event.

2. Use the ECHO to ECHO Technique to resolve several relevant events. The number of memories you will need to resolve will depend on the issue itself and the strength of the morphic field created.

3. With each of these memories, use the Classic Matrix Technique to resolve the trauma, find the negative belief and create a positive image, reimprinting any powerful new memories when applicable in the usual way.

4. When you feel the VoC level on the issue has decreased significantly, it's time to go to a future ECHO which has already achieved success in this area, i.e. has recovered from an illness, is enjoying a wonderful relationship, is financially successful, etc. Use one of the resolved memories. Step back into it and ask the ECHO to take you to a future self who is living this positive experience.

5. Upon finding this 'older you', elicit as much 'sensual' information as possible regarding the new picture, including sights, sounds, smells and touch. For example, if it's a beach scene, see the beauty of the landscape, hear the waves lapping the shore and the seagulls calling, smell the ocean and feel the sand beneath your feet and the warmth of the sun on your back.

6. What are the positive emotions you are feeling? (Joy, love, happiness, safety, connection?)

7. What are the colours around the picture?

8. What does this picture mean to you now? ('I'm successful and deserve this life.')

9. What else do you associate with this new situation?

10. Step into the ECHO of this amazing future and get a sense of what life is like. What are people saying? How does it feel to have resolved this issue? How does it affect other parts of your life? How does it affect people close to you?

11. Ask the future ECHO what advice you need to get to this point in your life.

12. When you have this full description, reimprint the memory.

13. After the reimprint, write a full description of all of the elements of the future memory. You may also wish to draw a picture of it.

14. Reimprint this memory every day for a minimum of 21 days, every night and every morning.

If the future memory doesn't feel congruent, it is a sign that more work needs to be done on the past. Ask this future ECHO where you need to go and do more work. This will lead you back down the ECHO stream.

As you're working through the 21-day process, you'll find the picture takes on a life of its own. This is fine as long as it's still positive. If you do feel something needs to be done about it, go back into the future-self memory and re-evaluate the situation to see what needs to change.

◆◆◆◆◆

Enhancing Your Work in the Matrix

As well as reading through this book and practising the enhanced techniques in this chapter, the following areas will complement your work as a practitioner.

Swap Sessions

This is the number one thing you need to do. It covers all of the following areas (training/practice/self-work and building a community). Swapping sessions with other practitioners is a major contributor to building confidence with the technique and benefiting from a support system as you work through your own issues. It also gives you a confidante if you'd like to discuss a client session.

Swapping is not just for the novice practitioner, it's for all levels. Indeed, experienced therapist Sally-Ann Soulsby told us that her weekly swaps with Erika Brodnock (contributor to Chapter 8) 'were invaluable in clearing blocks' to their success.

Here are some other comments we received from practitioners and trainers about the value of swapping sessions:

> 'From the day I trained in Matrix Reimprinting, I have held regular swaps every week or two weeks with some amazing fellow practitioners, always on Skype. It skyrockets your confidence for dealing with clients and you benefit from a regular way of clearing and uplifting your own life. There are amazing benefits to doing it regularly – like flossing, I guess!'
> CARYL WESTMORE

> 'Apart from the obvious, clearing my "stuff", I find it so valuable to have swap sessions for many reasons. I learn a lot from the other people's styles and techniques and it's good to be reminded of what it's like to be on the "other side" of the process. Although I know I can work on myself, I find working with my swap buddies allows me to relax into the process more. They ask different questions than I might ask myself, notice different things and find my "blind spots".'
> JEMA WRIGLEY

> 'Swapping keeps my energy flowing while untangling my personal patterns. The people I swap with inspire and teach me and I gain confidence with them, enabling constant learning. This allows me to give more to my clients. Also, feedback on these sessions is essential for our growth.'
> DENNY ELLIS

> 'In the past I've swapped Matrix Reimprinting sessions with people for reflexology and it was lovely to be worked on in a different way.'
> SARA MAUDE

Sara makes a good point, as throughout this book we're advocating a holistic approach to transforming your beliefs and your life. We want you to feel good, and if a massage is one way to raise your vibration, then find a masseuse who will swap with you. Kate has swapped Matrix Reimprinting sessions for personal training, chiropractic sessions, life coaching and more!

Training and Practice

The Matrix Reimprinting Practitioner Training will not only be an intensive two days where you will practise your skills in a live environment and watch Karl or one of his talented trainers in action, it will also be a space where you can explore your own beliefs. You'll leave this workshop with a new understanding of your life, what's in your morphic field and how you can begin to attract new experiences. You can read more about how to become a practitioner (which also gives you access to a huge swap list) at the back of this book (*see page 263*).

Karl has long been a supporter of his practitioners developing their own styles and niches, for example Sharon King with her successful Matrix Birth Reimprinting technique and Kate with her creativity and writing workshops. Attending the trainings of other practitioners who have developed niches will also bring new skills into your practice.

Practice

Here comes the cliché... yes, practice really does make perfect. Knowledge of ECHOs alone will not release their trauma, but actually using the Classic Technique will!

Also, as you spend more time communicating with ECHOs, you'll naturally develop your own style of working, including your favourite questions, reframes and description of the reimprinting process. As we've said before, it's a fluid process to which you'll bring your own expertise and life experience.

Self-Work

No matter how long you've been a practitioner or worked in the healing or psychotherapeutic field, a commitment to self-work is of utmost importance.

Working on specific beliefs or life themes is the way to get true resolution and move forwards with this technique. Most 'Matrixers' don't need reminding of this, because once you know how good it feels to be free of those old patterns, you can't wait to clear even more.

Building a Community

Matrixers are passionate about this technique and it's reflected in their online activity. There's a large group on Facebook as well as the Matrix Reimprinting social network, which is a hive of advice, activity and support.

You may also wish to run or attend local meet-up groups, work under supervision or have swap days to have contact with other practitioners face to face.

Part II
LIFE THEMES

INTRODUCTION

Think of this book as your garden shed full of tools for the different areas in your inner landscape. Which field do you want to work on and what seeds do you want to plant?

We've chosen to look at the areas in which people most commonly seek help. We've also interviewed Matrix Reimprinting practitioners around the world who've worked in these areas and have deep knowledge to share with you.

Each chapter includes a theme overview, common beliefs, case studies and questions for you to ask clients. You'll also discover nuances to the Classic Matrix Reimprinting Technique within each life area, especially in the Creating a Safe Strategy and Positive Belief Reimprinting steps.

The chapters are designed as starting points. We couldn't possibly cover everything about pain management or abuse, for example, in a few thousand words, but we can give you guidance based on what's worked previously. We'll present the research and offer some main pointers which you can use to discover what works for you and your clients.

We'll begin with conscious parenting, as understanding children and how we ourselves were treated as a child is at the very core of Matrix Reimprinting.

Chapter 8

CONSCIOUS PARENTING

*'One generation full of deeply loving parents would change
the brain of the next generation, and with that, the world.'*

CHARLES RAISON

Your children can be your biggest teachers if you let them. But there'll be times when your child looks like the enemy. Their actions will trigger you into fight or flight. You might say or do things that remind you of your parents or how you were as a child. You might itch to smack them, yell at them, put them on the naughty chair, shut the door on them and even run away from them.

Welcome to parenthood. Being a conscious parent won't mean you won't get triggered. But it will mean that you recognize behaviour that you don't like and take steps to address it. It's also about being a conscious *person* first and foremost so that you model how to manage your thoughts, feelings and emotions for your children.

Transforming our subconscious beliefs from our childhood is at the core of Matrix Reimprinting. As we connect with our childhood ECHOs, see what they needed and how they felt, and understand the beliefs they formed about themselves, it'll naturally give us more understanding about how our own parenting style affects our children. For example, if you're in the Matrix talking and tapping with a five-year-old ECHO who's just been smacked, you may vow that you'll never physically reprimand your children.

Where Does Parenting Start?

According to some cultures, parenting starts before there's even a twinkle in the eye. Aboriginal cultures have recognized the influence of the conception environment for millennia; prior to conceiving a child, couples ceremonially purify their minds and bodies.[1] Imagine if we lived in a society where the majority of couples consciously chose to conceive and created a loving, nurturing space for the arrival of a new life into the world.

In Thomas Verny's book *Pre-Parenting: Nurturing Your Child from Conception*, he states: 'It makes a difference whether we are conceived in love, haste, or hate and whether a mother wants to be pregnant.'[2]

Research suggests that what's going on in the lives of parents during the process of genomic imprinting has a profound influence on the mind and body of their child. It's widely accepted that toxins from smoking, drinking and drugs can be transmitted through the placenta and have harmful effects on the unborn baby. But what about the emotional state of the mother? There's a growing body of research showing that foetuses not only gain their nutrients from their mother but also their emotions and perceptions of the world around them. Studies have shown that newborns recognize nursery rhymes that have been played while they were in the womb. Even tabloid papers have claimed that depression starts in the womb.

The passing on of information from mother to foetus is nature's ingenious way of preparing the unborn child for what they'll meet outside the womb.[3] If a child is conceived by a mother who welcomes them, wants them, cherishes them from the moment they were first imagined, this energy is passed on to them. If, on the other hand, the mother is sending the message that the child is 'a mistake' or is worried about how she will cope, these chemical signals will also affect the foetus.

If a baby comes into the world unloved or unwanted, it is likely to have a large number of negative core beliefs from an early age. These can include 'The world is a dangerous place', 'I'm not wanted', 'I'm not good enough', 'I'm worthless', and so on. These beliefs can be the springs that turn into torrents.

Let's not forget that pregnancy and birth are transformative events for all concerned. Clearly, the more consciousness we bring to these transitions, the more we will grow and develop our potential for further transformation. We have all been born and we will all have formed some beliefs from the time we were *in utero* and perhaps before this point. Thankfully, we have the gift of Matrix Birth Reimprinting, developed by Sharon King. This protocol has helped thousands of people reconnect with their own birth experience and transform it to one that is safe, welcoming and full of love. Kate knows first-hand how giving birth naturally can be an intensely joyful and pain-free experience. Time and time again practitioners have told us that transforming their birth experience and time *in utero* has had a huge impact on their current belief system.

How we enter this reality does matter. It's important to clear any trauma from our own birth experience, our partner's birth experience and any triggers during pregnancy, and you'll find Sharon's details at the back of the book.

Parenting Guilt

Perhaps you're reading this with a gulp in your throat, remembering all the times you haven't parented consciously – times when your parenting style resembled a tired bear with a sore head rather than a happy, respectful parent who had enough self-love to nurture themselves and their children.

We know that sentences like 'From the moment of conception to six years of age, children are modelling their parents' behaviour and imprinting all of their core beliefs, beliefs which will form the blueprint of their lives and their own children's future parenting style' may trigger blame and guilt for some parents. But this chapter is *not* about blaming parents, it's about empowering them to rewrite a happier childhood and create a positive, conscious platform from which they can parent.

Being a parent will mean that you'll get angry at some point, that you'll lose it, that you'll feel inadequate, hurt, lost, lonely and afraid. Yet if you have the strength to realize what's happening and are prepared to look at your own childhood scars and heal them, both you and your child will emerge stronger and more capable of handling what life has in store for you.

Here's a note from Louise Hay which can help us understand why our children have chosen us:

'I believe that we choose our parents.

'Each one of us decides to incarnate upon this planet at a particular point in time and space. We have chosen to come here to learn a particular lesson that will advance us upon our spiritual, evolutionary pathway. We choose our sex, our colour, our country, and then we look around for the particular set of parents who will mirror the pattern we are bringing in to work on in this lifetime. Then, when we grow up, we usually point our fingers accusingly at our parents and whimper, "You did it to me." But really, we chose them because they were perfect for what we wanted to work on overcoming.'[4]

But let's also acknowledge that parenting is the hardest job in the world. Somehow we're meant to navigate between unconditional love and setting limits, imposing discipline and empowering our children to be themselves – and be happy doing it! Not to mention the thousands of educational approaches proclaiming they've found *the* way to raise well-adjusted, self-disciplined happy children. It can all get a little bit confusing.

Don't imagine that your children won't go through trauma – that's inevitable. Yet parenting from our conscious mind rather than our negative subconscious patterns will equip our children with the tools they'll need for their journey through life. Dr Laura Markham, a parenting coach, states in her book *Peaceful Parents, Happy Kids* that:

> '...even a devoted mother or father often inadvertently [emotionally] hurts or scars a child. This includes parents who adore their children, who would be completely heroic and self-sacrificing if the situation called for it. Why the gap between our intentions and our actions? The reason is that while we would never consciously hurt our child, so much of parenting, like every relationship, happens outside our conscious awareness.'[5]

And let's not forget that the children who have adults even thinking about how to parent them consciously are the lucky ones. Across the world there are millions of children who live in poverty, who go to bed hungry every single night, live off rubbish dumps, live and breathe war, are forced to fight, are drugged, regularly abused, alone and scared and see no way out.

As much as we want to help our own children and become more conscious in our parenting, this chapter is about helping all children in any way that we can, whether we are a parent or not.

We all have a responsibility to do this.

Matrix Reimprinting for Parents

We often parent the way we were parented, unless we change our subconscious behaviour and what is held in the morphic field. As Bruce Lipton so eloquently writes:

> 'The fundamental behaviours, beliefs, and attitudes we observe in our parents become "hard-wired" as synaptic pathways in our subconscious minds. Once programmed into the subconscious mind, they control our biology for the rest of our lives... unless we can figure out a way to reprogram them.'[6]

Luckily, Matrix Reimprinting gives us a way to do just that.

So, how do we do it? Every trigger is different and children can go from 0 to 10 emotionally in a split second. Here's a guide to how to navigate those triggers and some ways both we and our children can learn from them without the need for trauma:

✧ Tap for the parent.

✧ Diffuse the situation.

✧ Tap with the child.

✧ Take a Matrix break – surrogate tapping.

✧ Future Matrix work – clearing patterns from the past and for the future.

Tap for the Parent

When you become triggered by a child, use the basic EFT protocol to bring down the energy that you're feeling. This will give you a sense of control and enable you to focus on the situation by taking you out of the fight or flight response. When you bring yourself out of this response, everything changes.

Every parent knows that when they're feeling angry or frustrated, their children will be picking up on that energy and mirroring it back to them. So, in order to help our children, we have to take care of our own wellbeing first.

Diffuse the Situation

Once the situation has calmed down, analyse it, dissect it, work out what happened and notice when you were in the wrong. Own that 'wrongness' and go and apologize to the child if needed.

Think of them in terms of little ECHOs. How can you resource them? What do they need? As we know, it's often to feel safe and to feel part of a community – to get a hug from Mum or Dad.

Please note we're not telling you how to set limits for your child. This is an area you have to address yourself, bearing in mind your individual child's needs.

Tap with the Child

Children are already present – they're 100 per cent in the moment. When a traumatic incident happens, by using basic tapping we can release the flight, fight or freeze response immediately. We might not prevent an ECHO being created, but tapping allows the trauma to be resolved instantly, so there will be less energy and the situation won't hold such an emotional charge. This means that there won't be a build-up of ECHOs within a certain area or belief system. We can think of it as cleaning our mind as we go.

If we can encourage our children to heal themselves whenever they need to, they'll have fewer frozen ECHOs building up in their subconscious. We can make this process exciting for them by using language that's appropriate to their age and understanding.

First, introduce basic tapping to a child. The use of a tapping bear makes this a fun game and you can sew on the tapping points yourself. Much as traditional psychotherapy uses sandpit play or doll role-play to understand what a child is thinking, this works using transference: a child will transfer how they are feeling to the bear.

For older children, once tapping is established as a technique that helps them feel better, you can experiment with Time Travel Tapping. Forget calling it the Matrix or making it overly complicated. Generally speaking, children are much more imaginative than us adults – ask them to imagine a scenario or past situation and they're there.

A child's energy clears very quickly, as although they may have belief systems already in place, they're not compounded by the hundreds of reinforcing events that an adult will have in their field.

Meet Lily, a 10-year-old who didn't want to go on long car journeys. As the generalization effect began to occur, she became increasingly phobic about going in the car at all, and soon she didn't want to get the bus to school either.

Lily and her Matrix Reimprinting practitioner went into the Matrix and found an ECHO who had gone on a long car trip and returned home to find her dog had died. Around three to four weeks later, she had gone on another car journey and by the time she got back her grandmother had also died. So, within a short space of time Lily had undergone two major incidents and her belief was: 'When I go on car journeys, somebody is going to die.'

The other aspect to these events was the guilt she felt about the losses. Her parents had been encouraging her to be responsible for the dog and doing things such as walking it, brushing its coat and playing with it. She felt she hadn't been living up to their expectations and was absolutely distraught and overwhelmed with guilt when the dog died. Likewise she hadn't been to visit her grandmother for a little while and felt guilty about her lack of contact.

Prior to the first session Lily had a 10-minute school bus trip to a local swimming pool and was adamant she didn't want to go. After the first session, she managed the trip through gritted teeth. It was in the following two sessions that she and her practitioner discovered and released the guilt that she felt about the dog and her grandmother, and she was able to say goodbye to them properly. Being empowered to do that in the Matrix and create a special place for them all to be together transformed Lily's reaction and she no longer had any fear of going on car journeys.

The beauty of this case study is that healing the ECHOs shortly after the trauma has helped this young girl release these shocks without entering into adulthood as a potential agoraphobic.

Take a Matrix Break – Surrogate Tapping

When you're triggered, chances are you won't have time to take a Matrix break, so make a note to work on it at a later date, especially if it's a recurring trigger. You may choose to tune in to how the situation made you feel or bring it to mind and step straight into the picture. Either way, find the relevant ECHO from your own childhood and move through the Classic Technique.

In the Matrix, all selves, past, present and future, are accessible. It is the same with our children. There does need to be an access point of trauma to move into the Matrix, but it doesn't need to be related to the child.

Once you're in the Matrix you can bring your child in, communicate with them and tap on them to see how they feel about the situation.

> Meet Sadie and her 18-month-old daughter, Tamsin. When Tamsin was six months old, Sadie left her with a new childminder for two mornings a week over a period of a month. She had checked out the childminder's references and knew she had an Irish wolfhound, but the childminder had promised her that the dog would never be in the house when Tamsin was there.
>
> Like many new mums, Sadie was nervous about leaving her daughter and returning to work, and decided to visit the childminder unannounced so she could check up on the quality of care her child was receiving. When she arrived, the childminder looked worried and when Sadie went into the kitchen she found Tamsin strapped into a buggy, the television on and the dog pounding around the room. Immediately she froze, grabbed Sadie and left without a word, never to return.
>
> The worry that Sadie had about what harm might have come to her child ate away at her for over a year before she worked on it with her Matrix Reimprinting practitioner. They went back to the scene and tapped on Sadie for her guilt and fear that something else might have happened. The childminder had two teenage sons and Sadie had a deep fear that they might have abused her daughter in some way. In the Matrix, Tamsin

communicated to her mum that she'd been feeling scared as Mummy wasn't there. She had huge separation anxiety and they tapped together to reduce the intensity of the emotions they both felt.

By releasing her guilt, Sadie shifted to a new perspective. She also spoke to the childminder in the Matrix and took practical action by sending a letter to the local childcare board reporting what had taken place.

Tamsin reassured her that nothing else had happened, she'd just been missing her mummy. The relief Sadie felt was visible on her face. She'd moved from guilt to knowing she'd done everything a responsible parent would. As well as checking up on the childminder, she knew she'd only employed her for a very short period of time and she felt good that she'd taken action quickly and rectified the situation.

Future Matrix Work – Clearing Patterns from the Past and for the Future

When we work with family fields, we often find belief systems going back generations. Through the Matrix, we can facilitate profound transformative work. Not only can we go back and surrogate tap for grandparents to find the source of an ECHO stream, we can also go forwards and bring in future generations.

We can look at beliefs and cycles that are sometimes entrenched in families and passed on from one generation to the next. Some people believe that their family is cursed, for example, or that the women are unlucky in love, that they will have children young. Some families are full of clichés such as 'Keep your head down and get on with it.' We can all connect to the idea that our family has a belief system and we're part of it. Using Matrix Reimprinting we can find where this system was formed and imprint more empowering beliefs instead.

If it's clear that a certain belief is ancestral and the work takes us back through the generations, or past lives, then we can bring in future generations and future lives as well. For example, if we're working on the belief that we're 'not very clever' and find that it was given to our mother and grandmother, we can go back and work surrogately to transform and resource the ECHOs that need empowering.

Before imprinting the positive picture we can bring in all the future generations, such as our children and grandchildren, and ensure that they're not carrying that belief.

If we're working on issues that we've had with a particular child, it makes sense that while we're tapping in the Matrix and clearing what's going on for ourselves, we do some surrogate tapping for the child as well. When that issue is clear and no longer a trigger for either ECHO, we can go to the future and imprint a scene where the opposite is present.

Meet Jasmine, who attended a 13-week parenting course that Matrix Practitioner Erika Brodnock was running. This is Erika's account:

'Initially Jasmine was angry and hostile and didn't interact with the group much but did join in with the tapping circle. After a few weeks, however, she came in and announced that the tapping stuff was really working for her. She confirmed to the group that she had been addicted to class A drugs for a number of years and that she wanted to stop so that she didn't lose her children, as the threat of losing them along with everything else she had already lost in life was unbearable.

I used Matrix Reimprinting with Jasmine, who explained that the reason she used drugs was that when she was younger she'd fallen in love with a man who had raped her, beaten her, then forced her to prostitute herself. As her tears flowed, we went back to the first time she had been raped by him and worked on that ECHO. We closed that session having taken the ECHO to a place of safety and I offered to work with Jasmine the following day and thereafter weekly until she had been able to rewrite her past and transform her future.

Over the next eight months Jasmine and I worked together weekly on ECHOs that had been through some of the most traumatic things I had ever heard. Each week, no matter what the gravity of the trauma or the age of the ECHO, we were able to find resolution.

Jasmine had the core belief that she was dirty and soiled. This came up time and time again through her ECHOs and as we cleared and transformed that belief it was beautiful to see Jasmine begin to love and care for her body, health, hair and appearance. Soon her skin was less sallow and eyes less sunken as she gained weight and revealed a new identity.

By the time we drew our sessions to a close, Jasmine was a trained EFT practitioner, working with her children to transform as many memories as she could.

I called Jasmine just before submitting this case study as I hadn't spoken to her in several months. She is happy and well and has not used heroin or methadone since July 2010. Her children are also well and thriving and they have a mum they can look up to.'

Matrix Reimprinting's Effect on the Family
Parents Taking Time Out for Themselves

Those who practise tapping and Matrix Reimprinting and clear their issues and improve their energy flow are often capable of taking on quite a lot of responsibility. Whether that involves volunteering at a local charity, being part of a therapy hub, seeing 30 clients a week, carrying out creative projects, reading a billion self-help books or attending seminars and training courses, it can be exciting but leave the self-care tank drained. And if our self-care tank is empty, it'll affect every area of our life, especially parenting.

The first step is to check in with our basic human needs and see where we might need some additional support in our life. We all know the basics about how to increase our energy levels. Ensuring we get enough sleep, eating nutritionally balanced food, practising meditation, making sure we have a daily connection with source, having a massage and of course booking in sessions with swap partners can all have a transformative effect on both us and our children. Another way to reduce stress is to use basic tapping for 10 minutes a day.

In essence, we need to take some special time for ourselves. When we're frazzled from the daily pressures of life, we don't have the patience or energy to give to a child. If we fill up our own well of love on the other hand, we'll have more to give our family. Also, by doing this we're modelling behaviour that our children will copy.

(If you're feeling particularly stressed, the following chapter may hold some additional answers for you.)

Managing Emotional Wellbeing

This is a personal account of how EFT and Matrix Reimprinting helped a mother and her six children manage their emotional wellbeing:

'I'm the mum of six children. I've got a 19-year-old, 15-year-old, 13-year-old, 11-year-old and twins who are seven years old. Six years ago I was diagnosed with bipolar affective disorder and it was difficult to manage all of the children and my illness. It was an incredibly tough time, as I'd been bullied at work following a return from maternity leave and this had brought to the surface traumatic memories of being bullied as a child. I went into complete shock and my whole world began closing in around me. I left my place of work, unable to cope with the daily attacks, and went on to find out that my partner had been cheating on me, so left my relationship and faced the daunting task of being an unemployed single mother. It was the first time I'd been unemployed since the age of 18 and I just couldn't see a way out of the ever-extending black hole I seemed to be free-falling into.

Then came the diagnosis and the medication that made me feel completely numb. It was two years into my illness that I found EFT, NLP and Matrix Reimprinting, which was how I managed to turn my life around. Eighteen months after I began using EFT, NLP and Matrix, I went back to see the psychiatrist who had diagnosed me and explained what I'd been doing and how I was now feeling. He told me I could never have had bipolar affective disorder in the first place, as it was incurable. Having received that news, I was determined not only to continue to manage my own emotions and mental health, but to help others to do the same too.

I realized how much of an impact on my children my illness and all the trauma we'd faced as a family had had. They were very unsettled and there were complaints from school on a regular basis, although these became less frequent as my health improved.

I turned to the same methods that had helped me make such huge strides. These tools had helped me deal with all the negative feelings I'd had, together with the traumas that had contributed to my illness. Before I'd had these tools, I hadn't known how to deal with my unpleasant emotions, and I realized that my children hadn't learned how to either.

After doing lots of tapping with my eldest daughter, who was 12 at the time, I took her onto one of Karl's EFT and Matrix training courses to develop her own learning on the subject. The result was absolutely phenomenal! Grace had always been bright and done well academically, but having these skills took her to a new level. She literally started to ace exams and fire on all cylinders. Soon she was helping her friends deal with their emotions by using EFT and I saw the impact that was having on them as well.

Following Grace's success, my son Michael, who must have been about 11 at the time, took Karl's EFT and Matrix training as well. Since that point, they've just been able to manage things a hell of a lot better.

What I noticed was that the minute my behaviour changed and my outlook on life changed, I started to model different behaviour for my children, and then their behaviour changed and their outlook on life changed as well.

I also tapped a lot around all my children, so my youngest, the twins, were actually tapping at three. If her oldest sister annoyed her, one *of the twins would come and get her "tappy teddy" and say, "Grace annoying me," over and over again. By the time she'd tapped through three points, she'd be off playing again – it cleared instantly. Now, if she falls off her bike or does something similar she can come and find her tapping wizard, have a little chat and that's it. She clears it and gets on with her day.'*

Tools for Children
'I Wish I'd Known This as a Child'

What if we teach these skills to our children? What if they don't need to wait until they're in their twenties or thirties and have a meltdown or a disease before they learn them? What if they can heal their ECHOs as they occur?

Think back to the spring at the top of the mountain. That spring has always been there, just as children arrive in this reality along with all the events that they have to go through, all the learning that's part of their journey. As adults who are already here, our job is to soften the blows and equip them with enough self-worth to help them on their journey.

We can help them stem the flow of negativity in their lives before it becomes a white-water rapid and teach them to control the flow of emotions and create calm lakes in their mind.

Connection, Play and Stories

As we know, one way that beliefs become subconscious is through modelling behaviour, especially our parents' behaviour. Children will adopt poses, gestures and phrases that they see and hear their parents adopt. The most powerful way we can teach our children is through modelling the behaviour we want to see. If you want your child to tap, then tap; if you want your child to be calm, then calmness is your aim.

'The most powerful teaching is not what you say or do to them, but your state of consciousness at home. That's the very foundation for teaching your children. It has nothing to do with teaching; the foundation for transmitting consciousness is not even wanting to transmit consciousness to them, but to hold the space of presence as you interact with them at home.'[7]

Connection and Play

Michael Mendizza and Joseph Chilton Pearce's inspiring book *Magical Parent, Magical Child* makes it clear that play, not programming, is the key to optimizing the learning and performance of infants and children.[8] People who want to parent consciously know that play and connection help children feel loved and empowered to find their own way in the world.

We also like how Dr Barbara Fredrickson advocates a 3:1 ratio of positive vs negative emotions. This takes people to a tipping point beyond which they naturally become more resilient to adversity and effortlessly achieve what they could once only imagine.

Stories

A mother once brought her nine-year-old potential 'prodigy' son to Albert Einstein and asked how the boy could improve his mathematics. Einstein replied, 'Try telling him some stories.' The mother persisted in asking about the maths. Einstein said, 'Tell him stories if you want him to become intelligent, and even more stories if you want him to become wise.'[9]

Einstein knew that hammering a child with homework or flashcards was no way to cultivate a creative conscious mind that could think independently. When children hear stories, however, they look for a meaning that they can relate to their own life.

This is perhaps another reason why Matrix Reimprinting works so well with children, as it lets them tell their own interactive stories about what has happened to them. Play, stories, connection and awareness are some of the parenting tools we can develop alongside our tapping practices.

We may understand the need for conscious parenting. Yet we're still human, so we shouldn't expect to be perfect at parenting – particularly as the disappointment of not being perfect is going to have a far greater impact on our children than just accepting that we'll get things wrong sometimes. We also need to acknowledge that we don't own our children and they have their own journey to make.

When we do get things wrong (which we will!), being conscious is about putting our hands up, apologizing and moving on with a willingness to react differently in the future. This is true progress.

If you manage to do this, congratulate yourself for taking a step forwards and not operating out of your own subconscious programs and coercing a child from a place of fight or flight. It's not easy choosing to parent this way, but who said the evolution of the human race would be?

Chapter 9

MOVING THROUGH STRESS, ANXIETY AND DEPRESSION

'Anxiety is a thin stream of fear trickling through the mind. If encouraged, it cuts a channel into which all other thoughts are drained.'

ARTHUR SOMERS ROCHE

Stress. A word with which we can all identify. We use it as a noun, an adjective and a verb. Count how many times you hear it said in a single day – by you, your family, your friends and the media.

Apparently we should all be doing our best to avoid stress – in recent years it has been dubbed 'the silent killer' responsible for work-related illness, heart disease and much more. Stress gets a bad rap, yet a certain amount of it is good for us – it is, after all, one of the body's natural processes.

Historically, our stress response guarded us against real threats to our survival, such as a wild animal attacking us or our homes. As discussed earlier, we respond physiologically to stress through a system known as the hypothalamus-pituitary-adrenal (HPA) axis. Essentially, the body goes into survival mode, and adrenaline, cortisol and other stress hormones flood our system as energy is diverted to making our body and mind fast, strong and instinctive. When we're in fight, flight, freeze mode, the subconscious mind takes over and pulls out a pre-learned program. That program can be instinctive (we pull our hands out of a fire), part of a morphic field (we're afraid of falling) or indicative of a traumatized ECHO or belief system (we run away from all dogs due to a dog biting us when we were younger).

This response is great when we're being chased by a tiger, but not so great when the 'threat' is a modern-day equivalent such as taking an exam, having a job interview or being forced to sit in a room with family members with whom we don't get on. In these situations we need our conscious mind to be in charge, yet any negative emotion, whether it be anger, embarrassment or a feeling of being overwhelmed, can trigger the stress response.

There are times when we need that extra rush of adrenaline, such as when giving a presentation or stepping out of our comfort zone and trying something new. But as well as the HPA axis, the emotional responses to stress are largely due to the brain being driven from the more primitive 'reptilian' part, which is concerned with our survival. When we switch into this part of the brain, it stops the higher functions of the mind – empathy, logic and seeing the bigger picture – from playing a part. The more stressed we are, the less we're able to think clearly and logically. And add to this the physical signs of stress, such as dizziness, blushing, butterflies in the stomach, trembling, nausea, diarrhoea, tightness in the chest, tunnel vision, a dry mouth, muscle tension, excessive sweating and cold hands, and it's easy to understand how all clarity and logic can be lost in a stressful situation.

The Stress Spectrum

We can go in and out of the stress process at many points during the day. Look at the following diagram showing the stages of stress:

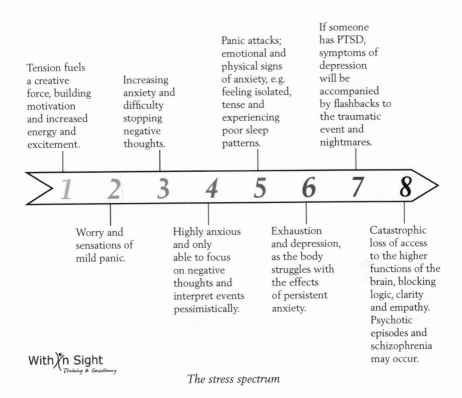

The stress spectrum

The following explains how each of the above stages might translate in the lives of two people – let's call them Simon and Marie.

Stage 1

32-year-old Simon keeps thinking about the presentation he has to give to his new boss. The thought makes him feel slightly nervous, creates 'butterflies' in his stomach and makes his hands clammy.

Stage 2

Mum Marie has a second child and starts to worry about money and how she looks. Her partner reassures her, but she continues to worry, She begins to feel isolated, has problems sleeping and becomes snappy.

Stage 3

Simon learns that there is going to be a series of redundancies, and starts to think they will be made on a 'last in, first out' basis. He loses sleep over the potential financial impact redundancy will have, and becomes tired and preoccupied with all the times in the past when life hasn't worked out. He fears he is a 'loser'.

Stage 4

Marie worries constantly, and is withdrawn and disinterested in the things she used to love doing. She spends a lot of time lying on the sofa, stressed and unable to think clearly.

Stage 5

Simon has a good review at work. He is given an important project to head up, but still thinks he is useless and will lose his job. Exhausted, he has his first panic attack and starts to dread going to work.

Stage 6

Marie gets support from her husband and best friend, but can't 'pull herself together'. She is unable to carry out day-to-day tasks, and feels she is living in a nightmare with no way out.

Stage 7

Simon can't enjoy his family as he is consumed by exhaustion and thoughts about work. He has a major panic attack at work, and is signed off by his doctor. His mind is a racing torrent of thoughts.

Stage 8

Marie and Simon have thoughts of suicide, and think others are going to harm them and believe their extreme thoughts to be true. Crippling anxiety and exhaustion fuel their misery and no one can get through the steel cage surrounding their negative thoughts.

We've all had days that are a one or two on the scale. We might have had days at a five or six, and survived longer periods of anxiety where we were operating at a four. Generally, we return to equilibrium after resolving the situation. The problem comes when these short-lived responses turn into chronic anxiety and permeate our waking thoughts.

Physical symptoms that can occur when stress is present for a longer period may include insomnia, waking exhaustion, headaches, musculoskeletal pain and problems with the gut such as constipation or persistent diarrhoea. The emotional symptoms that can appear in tandem are being unable to relax, having constant worrying thoughts, feeling overwhelmed, losing motivation, losing interest in previously loved activities, becoming tearful and emotional, and having fixed views and lowered concentration levels, together with a lack of self-esteem and loss of sex drive.

If we add in unmet human needs – such as a lack of connection – to this list of symptoms, we can see how chronic stress can affect our life on many levels. What can we do when anxious feelings become habitual? What if there is no respite from the stress? What are the links between stress, anxiety and depression?

Stressful Beliefs and Superhighways

All Matrix Reimprinting practitioners are experienced in managing the stress response. It's their job: to find what traumatized ECHO is causing the stress reaction and what beliefs are underpinning the response. Because under every pattern of stress, there'll be a core belief.

If we're running strong negative beliefs such as 'The world is a dangerous place', we'll look everywhere for proof that it's true. Soon we may see events that prove it everywhere we look, as we spend our whole life attracting and strengthening our core beliefs.

Based on these beliefs, we make good and bad generalizations. Many of our generalizations are useful; for instance we learn that working hard means that we will be successful. On one level we know that this is useful, and that if we are dedicated and motivated we will succeed. But what if our generalizations are making us stressed?

If we're running 'I'm scared of strangers', which is rather specific, it might initially stop us from going to places like bars or football matches. However, as we encounter more and more events that prove this belief to be true, we generalize our response to situations which 'feel' the same. The further we move up the stress spectrum, the higher our anxiety levels rise and the more our beliefs become generalized. This could result in us having additional beliefs such as 'People are judging me' and 'Strangers aren't safe' and eventually not wishing to leave the house and becoming agoraphobic.

We could look at anxiety about flying in the same way. Our first flight might have some turbulence which results in low levels of anxiety. The next time we have to fly we will be hyper-vigilant, looking for any signs of trouble (seatbelt lights, the looks on the cabin crew's faces, etc.), so more aspects (more energy) about that situation come in. If flying can't be avoided, the experience of these events can build up so that we have a complicated phobia about flying, underlying which is a fear of control, or of death in a vehicle that we're not controlling. This may then generalize to trains, cars, boats, etc. – all situations that feel the same, that have the same energy.

This is how we create 'stress superhighways' in our brain. If we think of our brain as a place with lots of roads, we can imagine a stressful situation leading us to a junction. We have the choice of turning left to the stress response or turning right to another way of dealing with the situation calmly. If we always turn left, that becomes the 'safe' way to react and soon we'll make the turn automatically and might even forget that there's an option to turn right, as that road has become overgrown and hard to find. What happens when lots of traffic uses a certain road? We extend it, we widen it, we build more road signs – and before long we have a 'stress superhighway'.

Meet Joe, a 15-year-old who was suffering from chronic anxiety, which was stopping him from attending school. With his practitioner he explored the patterns of anxiety, which had been set up on childhood holidays with his friends. Although Joe had looked forward to these holidays, when he visited his ECHOs they were wracked with guilt and anxiety about leaving his disabled mother and worrying about how she would cope without him.

His anxiety also stemmed from his first day at school and how afraid he was to be separated from his mother.

During the course of a year, Joe and his practitioner did some deep work on these issues and how every day at school had filed another ECHO in the subconscious drawer marked 'anxiety'. Interestingly, their work often led them back to three or four main ECHOs where this pattern had started, as there was so much learning and core-belief discovery about Joe and his mother's safety in the world.

Joe told his practitioner that understanding these anxiety triggers and releasing the stress through tapping 'flicked a switch' and after doing some sustained work he was able to return to school a happier, healthier young adult.

When Stress Moves into Depression

Think back to Diana and her journey of one belief: 'When things go well, I'll screw it up for everyone.' Over the years she'd proved this to be true and when she reached a particularly challenging time in her life, she was in a constant state of anxiety. Then she became depressed.

Depression is often a stress-related illness; the old term for it was 'nervous exhaustion'. There are also other causes of depression such as toxicity, or sensitivity to substances such as alcohol and drugs. It can also be part of another illness.

Depression is a giant problem both for the world and the individual who is struggling with it day to day. The 2004 *Global Burden of Disease* (GBD) report published by the World Health Organization (WHO) states: 'Unipolar depression makes a large contribution to the burden of disease, being at third place worldwide and eighth place in low-income countries, but at first place in middle- and high-income countries.'[1] Let that statistic sink in: in prosperous countries like the UK and USA, unipolar depression is the largest burden of disease – even over ischaemic heart disease (heart attacks) and cerebrovascular disease (strokes).

The symptoms of depression can be complex and vary widely between people, yet commonly include continuous low mood or sadness, feeling hopeless and helpless, having low self-esteem, lacking motivation or interest in things and feeling anxious or worried, along with slow movement and speech, changes in appetite, low energy, disturbed sleep and low interest in work, family and social interactions. These can be experienced alongside all the stress and anxiety symptoms outlined previously.

All of these symptoms begin to remove us from daily life. The more depressed we feel, the less we want to interact. It's a vicious cycle, as there is a need to withdraw from stressful situations, but this can make us feel isolated, which can then lead to deeper depression, and so on.

If we look at depression from the viewpoint of what the body is telling us, we can see that it's saying it needs to shut down and take us out of society to repair and heal. Just like the stress process, depression is meant to be a short-term adaptation.

We've all been on the spectrum of depression. We've all had hard times, sad times, bad times. If we've been healthy, we can be under high stress for some time and then emerge relatively unscathed. Not all stress and anxiety leads to depression, as you'll see in the following chapter. If, however, our body isn't healthy, is toxic and has a lowered immune system, and we have lots of strong negative beliefs, together with ECHOs from past traumas, then it may only be a short amount of time before depression kicks in.

Look at the spectrum (*see page 129*). Marie and Simon were coping with their anxiety at levels one to four, yet they both begin to have panic attacks and constant fearful thoughts about life when they hit number five. Our minds and bodies aren't capable of operating at these levels of anxiety and soon we become depressed.

If we then add secondary gains into the mix and other reasons to remain depressed, such as receiving love, sympathy and attention, or even becoming dependent on government benefits, we can see how hard it can be for some people to let go of the condition.

Depression and the Sleep Cycle

After collaborating with Jill Wootton, EFT and Matrix Reimprinting practitioner and solution-focused psychotherapist, we want to share with you how the sleep cycle and anxiety are a key part of understanding depression on a biological level.

If we're living in a stressed-out state, are generally anxious about life and can't find ways to release that worry by resolving the situation, then our brain has the emotional expectation that something bad will happen. Emotional expectations are enormously powerful in our day-to-day life. This is one of the reasons why placebo medication is so effective, because as well as working with our belief systems it also sets up an emotional expectation of future wellness.

Our brilliant body has a way of helping us manage our emotional expectations through dreaming, also known as Rapid Eye Movement (REM) sleep. Sleep researchers have known for a long time that depressed people dream deeper and longer than non-depressed people.

So, if we have excessive unresolved worries, stress and feelings of anxiety, it will lead to an increase in REM sleep. This has two major results:

1. If we discharge too much arousal in our sleep, we'll wake up tired.
2. Because of different bodily responses that are happening during the dreaming period, it will reduce our serotonin levels.

We almost wrote that second point in big capital letters, because understanding that excess dreaming also reduces serotonin, our 'satisfaction' neurotransmitter, is key in treating anxiety, stress and depression.

Serotonin Snapshot

Serotonin gives us a sense of satisfaction and helps us go into slow-wave sleep (as opposed to REM), which is the sleep we need for repair. It also helps us manage our emotional levels. For example, if someone steps on our toe, serotonin puts the brakes on so that rather than becoming completely enraged, we stop at mild annoyance. It also helps us feel socially confident, moderates our appetite, regulates our pain response and motivates us to move physically. The quickest way to generate serotonin is to exercise, which is part of that mind–body connection.

The reason that our level of serotonin is reduced when we're dreaming is because nature wants us temporarily paralysed (called catalepsy). Why? Although catalepsy is more complex than this, we need it because if we were motivated to move when we were dreaming, we might try to fly out of the window as Superman or attack our bed partner because we believed they were the bear in our dream. So, whilst we dream we have lower levels of serotonin. If we dream too much, though, we'll wake up with even lower levels of this vital hormone.

Key to stages of the cycle:
1. Worry about events, situations and people, past, present or future. Dominated by black-and-white thinking, and thoughts going round and round without ever being resolved. This causes high emotional arousal and chemicals such as cortisol and adrenaline to flood the body.

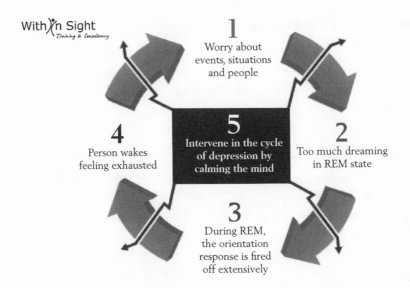

1
Worry about
events, situations
and people

5
Intervene in the cycle
of depression by
calming the mind

4
Person wakes
feeling exhausted

2
Too much dreaming
in REM state

3
During REM,
the orientation
response is fired
off extensively

The cycle of depression

2. Too much dreaming in REM state to try and resolve the emotional arousal. This eats into slow-wave sleep, which deprives the body of the restorative neurotransmitters, serotonin and dopamine.

3. During REM, the orientation response is fired off extensively. Someone who is depressed will dream about three times as much as someone who isn't.

4. Person wakes feeling exhausted and lacking in interest or motivation. They feel tired, and dominated by their emotional brain, and the cycle of worrying thoughts continues.

5. Intervene in the cycle of depression by calming the mind: Now you understand what causes depression, you can also see how the cycle can be broken. Any treatment that helps to calm negative rumination cuts excessive REM and increases slow-wave restorative sleep; this leads to increased energy and motivation on waking in the morning. EFT, Matrix Reimprinting, calming hypnosis, meditation, stabilizing blood sugars and making sure that basic needs are met will all help to calm a ruminating mind.

Calming the Mind Down

Working with chronic anxiety and depression can be like a bowl of spaghetti where all the issues and beliefs are looping in and around each other and it can be hard to know where to start. Let's begin with the basics.

Human Needs Check-in

All of us are born with basic physical needs such as the need for air, water, food and sleep. Without them, we quickly die. The European Therapy Studies Institute (ETSI), a multi-disciplined organization which pools together studies and publishes information on therapeutic methods and practices, has compiled, through research across gender, race and location spanning over a decade, a list of basic human needs that are vital for us to thrive. In fact our behaviour is driven by seeking to meet these needs.

The ETSI studied people who seemed to be examples of human excellence and found that their basic human needs were met at a high level. They also discovered that if one or more of the needs was not consistently met, one of four things usually happened: either the person would have an accident (even if it seemed completely random), or they would get ill physically, or they would develop a mental health problem, or they would revert back to old addictive patterns relating to alcohol, drugs, gambling, sex, etc.[2] If we can't get our human needs met in healthy ways, we eventually resort to less healthy ways – hence the reversal to old addictive patterns.

This body of research has gone on to form a foundation of the Human Givens Institute and their framework for psychotherapists.[3] We were first introduced to this work by Sally-Ann Soulsby, an experienced psychotherapist who is dedicated to building a bridge between the traditional and Matrix Reimprinting approach to therapy.

It is obviously important to know what these needs are, otherwise it's like playing football in the fog – if we can't see the goal, we're not going to score.

Furthermore, if we can combine our understanding of the belief system with the human needs inventory, we are giving ourselves and our clients the best chance of breaking free of anxiety and depression and thriving.

Have a look at the list of human needs below. Although not a definitive list of all our human needs, when we ask clients to fill in an inventory like this we're building rapport and also a picture of their home life.

Basic Human Need	Examples	How well is this need currently being met? Score 1–10 (1=not met at all; 10=fully met)	How will you better meet this need in the future?
The need to feel understood and connected	Sharing ideas, feelings and dreams with others		
The need to give and receive attention	Regular connection with other people		
Taking account of the mind–body connection	Exercise, nutrition and sleep		
Having a sense of control	An appropriate sense of control in your life, and letting go of things outside your control		
The need for creativity and stimulation	New challenges, learning and expanding your horizons		
The need for purpose and goals	Making future plans or having a sense of purpose		
A sense of connection to something bigger than oneself	Religion, community groups and voluntary work. Anything that takes the focus off yourself.		

Meet Linda, a teacher feeling stressed out by her job. Her practitioner questioned her about activities that brought her joy and she said that she used to love making cakes. Together they set some fun goals around making cakes again when she had some time off at the weekend.

Soon she was feeling much better and more rounded about life: 'I can't believe the difference just doing that has made. It's reminded me how much I love it. In fact I wish I'd done this as a career.'

Often people believe that taking time out for their own creativity or goals is a luxury that they can't afford. However, when we know that it's part of sustaining a healthy mind and living a well-balanced life, we can give ourselves permission to make the time.

With regards to depression and anxiety, it is vitally important to look in detail at the basic need of 'taking account of the mind–body connection' including 'exercise, nutrition and sleep'. We can't discuss anxiety and depression without mentioning these variables and the effect they have on our emotional, physical and mental states.

We all know that good nutrition is vital for the wellbeing of our body and that some types of food, such as starchy carbohydrates or sugary foods, will create peaks in blood sugar levels and create mood swings, which are the enemy of the anxious or depressed person. The inevitable crash from high-sugar foods creates an increased likelihood of craving more quick-release foods, thus creating a vicious cycle. We would advise everyone struggling with anxiety or depression to research nutrition and how they can improve their current diet.

Working with Chronic Stress and Anxiety

Looking at patterns of anxiety and depression, we can see that the way to break the stress cycle is to calm the mind down. This stops the anxiety, which in turn reduces the amount of REM sleep and soon energy levels will return to normal.

A mind full of traumatized ECHOs will be causing stress, so use the Classic Technique to find the relevant ECHOs and release any trauma that is held there.

Using a structure to rate beliefs and taking a human needs inventory can be a good place to start when working with chronic stress and anxiety – but the energy of the anxiety will always take it back to specific memories.

As we know, we'll all be on the stress spectrum at some point in our life. It may be because of a single event or belief, or it may have become generalized so that we feel anxious or worried about every area of our life. There is a difference between being anxious about a current situation or relationship and feeling permanently worried about work, children, health and relationships.

Amy is the mother of two children. In her first session she told her practitioner she was dealing with a consistent low-level sadness and bouts of debilitating depression. Over the next four months they worked with Matrix Reimprinting and found a core belief of 'It's not OK to show emotion and I should never tell people what's wrong.' This was twinned with the idea that Amy had to soldier on regardless of how awful she felt.

Using the Following the Energy technique, she connected with a younger ECHO who was visiting her mother in the hospital after she'd given birth to her little sister, and the ECHO had lots of feelings of being 'unloved'. Under the gentle guidance of her practitioner Amy released this trauma and imprinted a new picture.

At the end of the first session, Amy remarked that she was going to allow her husband to take more of the parenting responsibility, though she found it hard to let him in. They revisited the memory and connected with her husband's ECHO and he was delighted to be able to parent more.

A key memory that they discovered was of Amy being on holiday in Spain as a teenager and out in the local town with her sister, who had severe asthma. A bunch of local kids who hated tourists started chasing them both through the streets. To avoid her sister being chased and possibly having an asthma attack, Amy drew the boys towards her instead. She was terrified that her sister would have an asthma attack, but in fact her sister managed to get away and speak to some adults, who got her father to come and rescue Amy. Eventually the boys were scared off, but Amy had been hit and was in pain and very upset. Once the other adults were out of sight, her father started to beat her, saying it was her fault.

Amy entered the memory at this point of trauma and removed the ECHO from her situation. They went to a calm beach and after tapping on her ECHO, she told Amy that she needed a hug and to be told that she wasn't in the wrong. Gradually, over about five minutes, the ECHO calmed down and was open to the idea that someone else could have a word with Dad to find out why he'd reacted that way.

The ECHO of her husband came in and spoke to her dad on the other side of the beach. The younger ECHO could see her father being really gentle with him. He put his hand on his shoulder and just listened. Her dad said he was so sorry and was very upset. What he needed was his own mother to comfort him. They brought the spirit of his mother in, who was loving and kind and said she could do now what she'd not been able to do before.

They tapped on Dad's sadness and sense of being overwhelmed, and eventually Amy's ECHO felt safe enough to go over to him. He told her that he'd never been able to cry in front of anyone, so whenever he saw her cry, he went into a blind panic and did anything to stop her crying, even beating her. Through all of these realizations, she was able to understand his perception and forgive him. Eventually she was able to sit on his lap and have the cuddle she needed, feeling his big strong arms around her.

Over their sessions together, they also worked on memories of being in hospital and being alone. There were also several more times when her ECHO had been beaten by her father.

The belief that ran through all of these events was 'I should not tell people what's wrong.' Yet over time Amy had Matrix Reimprinting sessions, she built the strong belief that it was safe to share how she felt with those around her. Through this she was able to communicate with her partner and her children about the sadness and worry she'd been feeling and felt much lighter as a result. She finally had some recognition of how greatly she was loved. She'd never seen or felt this before.

At the end of the four months, Amy told her practitioner, 'I feel my life is unfolding and am feeling really positive. I'm able to stand my ground when others challenge me in a way that I could never do before.'

Another positive outcome was that Amy had more confidence in her own parenting skills and ability to be calm with her children.

Whatever stress or anxiety is invading your life, here are some insightful questions and steps that you can use to monitor your (or your clients') progress.

Stress and Anxiety

Insightful Questions

1. 'How much does stress affect your life?'

'Out of 100 per cent, with 100 being "it totally dominates" and 10 being "it's only a slight problem", how much is this stress/anxiety a problem in your life?'

2. 'What are the symptoms?'

'What are the exact physiological symptoms and how intense do they get out of 100?'

If there are lots of symptoms, make a note of the scores separately, e.g. racing heart: 75 per cent; sense of dread: 60 per cent; etc. This will give you a marker for progress and help you access the memories in the Matrix by Following the Energy.

(If working with a client, it's important to assess their progress over a series of sessions with these first two questions.)

3. 'When is the condition triggered?'

'What issues, thoughts, challenges, life situations, comments and so on trigger the condition?'

Be clear and make notes. You can use these times to get back to the Matrix and find memories.

4. 'What are the consequences of having this condition?'

'What actually happens in your life as a result of the anxiety, such as not going to meetings or social gatherings, or phoning in sick for work?'

This will highlight any themes or secondary gains, and also provide a marker for improvement.

Steps

- ✧ Have a list of symptoms and when they're triggered, you can tune in to the energy of one symptom or of how that situation feels.

- ✧ You can then use the Classic Technique to trace back to the ECHO that is triggering this response.

It's best to work on a specific symptom for a while, completely clearing the root or belief behind the reaction before you move on to another symptom. Don't look for a 100 per cent improvement, but the issue does need to be significantly clearer before you move on.

You can also go straight to significant events. If there was an event in your life that causes you stress and anxiety when you think about it, it means it is a live event in your subconscious, a traumatized ECHO in your field. These are the traumas to start clearing straight away.

◆◆◆◆◆

Future Work
Positive Belief Imprinting

Jemima Eames is an experienced practitioner who has specialized in helping people manage their anxiety and stress levels. She finds that one of the most important aspects of a 'stress-relief' session is to ensure that the client walks out of the door a little bit lighter, with one area of stress in their life completely transformed.

One way of doing this is through using the Positive Belief technique. Although we do want to ensure that we clear a fair amount of trauma and trapped negative energy before going to a future self, by helping the client to imprint a good feeling at the end of the session you're setting up a new neural pathway.

Remember those stress superhighways? Imprinting a future image is like setting a location on a map and then using a satellite navigation device to find it. Jemima also encourages her clients to buy a scarf or a piece of jewellery or a picture frame that's the colour of that future self and to put it up somewhere where they can see it all the time to embed that future energy.

Calming the Mind Down: A Stress-Relief Toolbox

Often people walk through a practitioner's door desperate for a new tool to ease that traffic flow and manage their stress and anxiety levels. Perhaps they've read some literature on tapping and have had some great results, but want to get to the core of their issues. Doing a rating on symptoms and belief scales and checking in with the human needs checklist, we can begin to piece together a picture of how much stress, anxiety or depression is part of their life.

Our job as practitioners is to help people navigate their stress levels both in and out of the sessions. In the area of stress management and depression, homework between sessions is of utmost importance, because the stress responses may already be superhighways and have strong morphic fields, therefore it can take sustained work and commitment to clear them.

Imagine a cat has got a ball of bright pink wool and been playing with it, tangling it all up. But you need that wool to make a beautiful jumper for yourself and begin to unravel it slowly and mindfully.

Bear in mind that there will be areas of life that will improve more quickly than others, especially if you use the emotional inventory alongside a checklist of beliefs. What about the rest?

Creating a stress-relief toolbox that's tailored to your needs is 10 times more powerful than advice from others. It gives a feeling of control – you don't have to wait for an appointment or someone else to help you. Having your own tools and techniques to use whenever and wherever you like is much more effective. Even if you have to use them 20 times a day, they'll still be working and you'll be soothing yourself and taking back control of your life. In your toolbox you might have:

✧ Tapping as a daily stress-relief tool. This helps manage the stress response and brings clarity and perspective. Tune in to the energy, describe it and tap on it to release it from the body. This will begin to train the brain. It will demonstrate that the brain has options other than zooming directly to the stress response.

✧ Meditation, self-hypnosis and visualization are all tools that help to calm the mind. However, telling a highly stressed person to go and sit quietly in a state of meditation can actually make it worse! Always start where the client is. Research short meditations, Smartphone apps for sleep, creative visualizations and relaxations.

✧ Heart breathing – spend five minutes a day doing this breathing exercise (see page 69).

✧ You can also record the imprinting part of your session to listen to and visualize in between sessions.

✧ Continually check in with the human needs inventory and rate the mind–body connection. Exercise and nutrition are vitally important.

✧ Some practitioners also encourage clients to write down their anxious feelings in a journal, as this enables them to express often stockpiled emotions whilst still awake and thus takes the pressure off having to dream the emotions at night. You may also like to suggest that clients tap whilst rereading their journal entries.

How Long Will It Take?

Treating anxiety and depression can take time. As we've said before, there is a spectrum. If there's a single event or belief underpinning the behaviour, then it can be a much shorter process. However, depression can be very serious and we strongly recommend that people who are in a deep depression only work with Matrix Reimprinting practitioners who have the relevant skills and experience.

> Meet Peter, a 62-year-old man who, as far back as the age of 12, had always felt he was separate from everybody and that no one cared about him. This feeling continued until he had a breakdown in his late teens when he went to university, and during his twenties he took a cocktail of antidepressants.
>
> Over the next four decades he admitted himself to the authorities for sectioning no fewer than four times. During this period he had a marriage breakdown and also took many more combinations of prescribed medication.
>
> In his fifties he met the love of his life and they had a child together. During these few years the depression lifted, but then it came back again.
>
> It only took three sessions to clear this heavy depression, as client and practitioner found an early ECHO from which it all stemmed.

Peter was about 10 years old at the time and attending a local boarding school, which meant he went home every weekend. When his ECHO was dropped off at the school gate, all he could hear was his mother's footsteps walking away from him. Peter was off the scale with anxiety recalling this. His ECHO's belief was that he wasn't wanted and that his mother had sent him away to school because his younger brother was 'better'. He felt unloved and not good enough. The trauma of leaving his family every Sunday night and the feelings of anxiety about this had pervaded every aspect of his life. He shook when he spoke about it.

Although there was no 'big T' trauma during his time at school, his sensitive little ECHO was completely traumatized by being apart from his family.

Peter had spent the rest of his life trying to be 'interesting' and make people like him. The anxiety around the belief 'People don't want me around' had affected all areas of his life – his work, his relationships, his marriage – so new situations and life changes often sent him spiralling into chronic anxiety and depression.

By working with these ECHOs and understanding this belief, he connected the dots and was finally free of its grip. He released all the energy held by those ECHOs and created stronger beliefs to help him move forwards in life. The practitioner also worked with the human needs inventory and through this Peter rediscovered his love of cooking.

When it came to Peter's fourth session, he called his practitioner and cancelled it, saying, 'I'd love to see you, but I don't need it, as things are improving day by day. I feel so happy and content.'

As we can see from the case studies in this chapter, understanding how we manage our stress levels and emotional wellbeing with regards to our beliefs is key to preventing patterns of anxiety and depression.

What if we all became better at managing our stress levels? What if we saw rising stress and anxiety as a way of finding out more about ourselves? What if we embraced these reactions and saw them as a way into our inner landscapes? What if we used 'stress' to find our core beliefs and transform them into supportive platforms?

If we can move through stress and anxiety in our life, we can move through anything, including depression. Matrix Reimprinting and EFT will calm the mind down and help us find new routes in the brain. Let's move from that Friday afternoon motorway traffic to calmer lanes with a view of the countryside!

Chapter 10

MANAGING PAIN IN THE MATRIX

'Pain can be endured and defeated only if it is embraced. Denied or feared, it grows.'

DEAN KOONTZ

We'll all experience physical pain at some point in our life, but why do people experience such different pain levels? Pain is subjective and two people with the same condition will experience it completely differently. For example, take two people who have whiplash, an injury that affects the neck. One person may heal and be pain-free in six weeks, whilst another may have a lifetime of chronic pain. Why is that? These two people won't be that biologically different – none of us are. We all have billions of cells that are the same and our major organs operate in exactly the same way. Yet we heal differently. Why?

The difference is in the flow of signals or messages to and from the brain, but what are messages if not the energy flowing around our body – our thoughts, feelings, emotions and, yes, beliefs? Matrix Reimprinting works with those signals, that energy, and it can be like turning off a switch and stemming the flow of pain.

In this chapter we aim to give you a brief overview of how we can use the Classic Technique with different types of pain, together with some insightful questions and helpful pointers. Furthermore, we draw on the Meta-Health research and outline a diagnostic approach to releasing pain in the musculoskeletal system.

How to Work with Pain Using Matrix Reimprinting Classic Technique

If someone walks through the door in pain, do you think you should be talking about beliefs? Their entire life story? About how all pain is a signal from the brain? No way! A practitioner's job is to work with the pain first. If we can help someone with pain relief, we've opened the door to other possibilities in their mind. It's also a powerful demonstration in a group setting or when we want to show people how to work with the energy in their body.

In order to help categorize pain for you or a client, you could use the questions below, as the answers may give some clues about what the pain might be related to.

Insightful Questions to Ask

1. 'When did the pain start?'

2. 'Do you take medication?'

3. 'What's your overall goal in terms of pain relief?'

4. 'How intense is your pain on a daily basis on a scale of 1 to 100, with 0 being "no pain" and 100 being "maximum pain"?'

5. 'Are there certain times during the day when your pain worsens, suddenly disappears or gets better?'

6. 'Are there certain situations that trigger your pain? If so, please explain.'

7. 'Is your pain or injury the result of trauma?'

8. 'Have you been to see a doctor about your pain or injury? If so, what was the presenting problem?'

9. 'What are your symptoms?'

Basic Tapping

Because pain isn't an esoteric notion and is felt right there in the body, it's easy for people to tune straight in to it and describe how it feels to them.

✧ Use the basic EFT protocol to break the pain down. Use colours and textures and describe the pain in detail. Is it burning? Probing? Stabbing? For example, someone may have a 'red angry stabbing pain in my shoulder'.

✧ Then do a few rounds of tapping to bring the intensity down. You may need to chase it around the body as you do so. For example, the 'red angry stabbing pain in my shoulder' may become 'a pink sludge sliding down my back'. Continue tapping to reduce the intensity.

✧ You can also ask 'What is the opposite of this pain?' Perhaps it is 'peace' or 'relaxation'. Use this as a reframe in the EFT process.

When someone has chronic or long-term pain, teaching them basic EFT early on can help them manage it in between sessions. Bear in mind that long-standing pain that has a dense field may take longer to clear, especially when you consider potential secondary gains that might be in place.

◆◆◆◆◆

✧ Once you've gained a description of the pain, listen out for key phrases such as 'being stabbed in the back' and ask, 'If someone or something was stabbing you in the back, who or what might it be?' Give them time to answer. When they reach a specific memory, move to Step 1 of the Classic Matrix Technique.

✧ The other key question is: 'When was the first time you felt this pain?' This may lead you to the trauma when the pain started and you can go back into the memory and clear the ECHO's trauma.

✧ The emotion of the pain is important. Ask, 'If this pain had an emotion attached to it, what would it be?' Ask probing questions related to the emotion of the pain, such as 'If there were someone or something you felt angry about, who or what might it be?' or 'If there were someone or something you felt guilty about, who or what might it be?' You can then build up a picture of what's happening in their life that is affecting this part of their body. It may be a recent event. Start there and clear that energy first.

✧ Personify the pain by asking questions such as 'If your pain had a message, what would it be?' or 'If this pain reminded you of someone or something, who or what would it be?' or even 'If this pain had an identity, who or what would it be?'

By asking questions and gathering information you'll soon find an event or memory. You may even wish to personify the pain and treat it as you would an ECHO, tapping and releasing any negative emotions that the character is holding on to.

The information that comes up will help you build a picture of what is happening in a client's life and what may be underpinning their pain.

◆◆◆◆◆

Types of Pain

When working with physical pain, it can be helpful to categorize the type of pain that is present.

1) Pain as a Result of Trauma (either Real or Imagined)

All pain is the result of trauma, whether physical or emotional in nature, but, to be more specific, we may know exactly what trauma triggered this pain in the first place.

This is often the easiest one to work with, as straight away there will be a memory present and we can go in and clear the energy from the ECHO. As the energy may be stuck in the ECHO, it can be released from just one memory.

Meet Gerry, a 52-year-old man with lower back pain. When his practitioner questioned him about the beginning of the pain, he realized that it had started when he'd changed jobs a couple of years earlier. He'd put it down to his previous job as a postman being physical and keeping him quite fit and his new (part-time) job as a delivery driver being much more sedentary. However, after using some basic EFT, he realized the emotions that he associated with the pain were frustration and some sadness. He was initially confused about this, but with gentle questioning was able to trace it back to feeling that he wasn't up to the job of being a postman any more.

He and his practitioner went back to an ECHO at his leaving party who was feeling sad and alone as he was leaving a job he'd held for 15 years and had the underlying belief that he was 'past it'.

He tapped on his ECHO, releasing all the emotions and reassuring him that life would get better and that his new job would be fantastic. The ECHO felt empowered about his new job and saw it as an opportunity to move forwards into the next phase of his life, as well as receive higher wages and be able to have a coffee when he liked!

Not only did this session help Gerry's back pain, but it also gave him a renewed joie de vivre and he started planning some worldwide travel to places he'd always dreamed of visiting.

2) Pain as a Result of a Physical Injury

What is a physical injury if not trauma? Yet why do some people heal faster than others? Using Matrix Reimprinting we can find the event, move the ECHO safely through the trauma and help the body heal itself. When we revisit a memory that involves a physical injury, it's important to release all of the trauma from the ECHO and focus on this during the reimprinting stage.

As we discuss in the latter part of this chapter, approaching the issue diagnostically enables us to understand why that particular part of the body is under stress or weaker in the first place.

3) Pain as Part of a Complex or Serious Disease

When working with serious disease, there will be different symptoms at different times, with many beliefs and traumas. We can break down the pain into specific areas or symptoms and work with one at a time to clear the energy stream behind it.

Matrix Reimprinting can truly aid recovery from a serious disease, whether predominately physical or psychological, especially when it is used in tandem with analysis of the body's messages. However, the road to recovery from a serious disease can be long and complex. Clients will need guidance on elements like nutrition and self-love, and above all they will have to commit to doing self-work in between sessions with their practitioner.

Of course we want to get to the core issues and beliefs, but dealing with symptoms, such as managing pain levels, is a great place to start, and this can really assist the client in terms of helping them manage their energy system and give them hope for the future.

In *Matrix Reimprinting Using EFT*, there is extensive coverage of how to work with serious disease.

4) Pain as a Primary or Secondary Gain

Primary and secondary gains are reasons why a person is holding on to their pain. It could be a way of gaining love or attention. It could be the excuse they 'need' to not function properly in their life. It could be their way of expressing anger and resentment about someone else. For example, they might not want to forgive the person that they believe caused the pain in the first place.

This is a sensitive area that needs careful consideration before questioning a client, especially when working with chronic pain and/ or serious disease.

Primary Gain

A primary gain is when the pain serves a fundamental life purpose, so the body remains ill to continue serving this purpose. When working with a client, ask questions about any upsides or positive aspects to having the pain. Common beliefs can be around teaching other people to be careful with them, so the pain is working as protection. It can also be linked to getting attention and love or having more time to do what they want. This is an area in which to tread carefully. People may have a deep and inherent reason for holding on to their pain.

> *Master Meta-Health trainer Rob van Overbruggen was working with Mary, who had shoulder pain. She told him, 'Whenever I'm at home, I have to be doing something for the household, whether that's cleaning, taking out the rubbish, fixing something or cooking. It's not OK for me to sit down and have a cup of tea for five minutes.'*
>
> *Rob instructed her to take 15 minutes off every day and sit in her room and meditate. He even wrote a note to her family saying it was vital for her to do this. After one week of taking 15 minutes a day for herself, she found the shoulder pain had gone. There was no reason for it to stay.*

Secondary Gain

Secondary gain is when the pain fulfils a purpose on a level that isn't the main reason for being ill. When the underlying stresses and fears are resolved with Matrix Reimprinting, a person is often able to release and move through the subconscious secondary gains that keep the body in pain.

There is also the cycle of chronic pain and feeling helpless, for example if the person feels that they're letting people down or can't contribute to the family. These thoughts and feelings soon begin to create self-worth issues in their own right, which can lead to further pain.

For a practitioner, this is an extremely sensitive issue to raise. Do so only when you have been working with a client for some time and have built rapport and a safe environment. Keep in mind that secondary gains are subconscious and are often driven by a need to be loved and connected.

Assessing Gains

The key to exploring the possibility of primary and secondary gains is using a light and investigative manner rather than alienating your client by sounding judgemental or accusatory. You can add to your list of insightful questions by creating rapport to find out how the pain has affected their life and how they feel about themselves as a result of it.

Here are some questions to help you determine whether primary or secondary gains are in play:

✧ 'If there were an important reason for keeping this pain, what would it be?'

✧ 'What purpose does this pain serve?'

✧ 'If this pain went away tomorrow, what would you have to do that you don't like doing?'

✧ 'Are you remaining in pain for someone else's benefit?'

When people are ill, they often end up playing roles in a partnership and it's sometimes more challenging for someone to get well when they are in a couple, or part of a family dynamic, than when they're on their own. Explain this and ask, 'If this were to apply to you, how would it work?'

Working with Long-term and Chronic Pain

Meet Gemma, a lady in her mid-thirties who had reflex pain dystrophy (RSD)/chronic regional pain syndrome (CRPS) for almost a decade. In her words:

'For the past nine years the thought of something even slightly touching my left arm/forearm made me cringe and feel sick. The sensitivity was unbearable. That's because being diagnosed with RSD/CRPS left me on a roller-coaster of unbearable pain, extreme sensitivity to touch, shakes, spasms, anxiety, panic attacks, depression and insomnia.

'I'd been in remission for a couple of years, where the pain subsided but the sensitivity remained, then in 2009, after the birth of my son, Eddie, my symptoms came back worse than ever before, with the RSD/ CRPS spreading to the left side of my face and left eye and leaving the entire left side of my body too sensitive to be touched or hugged. I also started collapsing, having blackouts (recently diagnosed as vertigo) and having difficulty coordinating my left leg/foot, which left me unable to walk very far and also needing to use a walking stick. It became impossible for me to take care of Eddie on my own, which left me even more determined to get better and beat RSD/CRPS a second time.

'This time around none of the treatments (nerve block injections, physiotherapy, acupuncture) worked. The only thing that seemed to keep me going was the medication, so the doctors just kept adding more and more to the mix and giving me it at the highest doses. It seemed that the more determined I was to get better, the more the doctors advised me to expect the worst. A previous therapist even explained to me that as I was "unable to accept" my condition I would never be able to move on. ("How will I ever move on in this terrible

pain?!" my head screamed!) A close family member said to me, "Accept that your life is different now. You will never be able to work again, the old Gemma is gone and you must get used to this new life of RSD and learn to cope." (But my head screamed, "No!")'

Gemma worked with Matrix pain specialist Carey Mann, who gently guided her back to Eddie's birth, when she had relapsed. Gemma connected with her ECHO and tapped on all the pain and fear.

When that was cleared, in order to make the ECHO less fearful, Gemma explained to her that the outcome would be fine – her son would be OK. As the birth was taking place in Spain, she made her feel safer by having people speaking English.

When the ECHO was in a place of workability, it emerged that the belief that she had was that she was 'weak' and 'couldn't cope' and she had some 'negative feelings about creating a family', believing 'it will all go wrong'. Through showing the ECHO that actually she was going to be OK, her son would be fine too, her little family would be wonderful and it wouldn't all go wrong, Gemma was able to help her feel stronger and able to cope. In order to boost that feeling of confidence she referred back to a time when she was living in California and had an amazing feeling of confidence and self-worth, which she imprinted.

At the end of the session (which was the first they had had together and Gemma's first experience of EFT), Gemma remarked that the pain and sensitivity had completely gone from her hand and forearm. Not long afterwards, she followed her session up with a testimonial for Carey to use:

> 'It wasn't until I was on the train home that it began to sink in just how successful the EFT had actually been. In fact I think I was still in shock!… There I was sitting on the train actually wearing my wedding ring on my left hand as well as my watch on my left wrist, something I hadn't been able to do since 2004. My husband couldn't believe it either – we both sat staring at my hand!'

Gemma continued to work with Carey and had around 10 sessions. She was committed to doing self-work with EFT and understood the beliefs and mind–body connection. A few months later, she added the following to her testimonial:

> 'Since meeting Carey I've completely come off my medication and I'm so much brighter and happier! After that first session my walking went back to normal and I haven't had to use a walking stick since. I've even started walking for fitness and walked six miles last Monday! Best of all, though, is the look on my son's face when he comes out of school and sees me there waiting for him and we walk home together, just the two of us.

> 'I still have RSD/CRPS in my face and the vertigo still flares up sometimes, but my symptoms are under control now. My pain used to be an eight constantly, flaring up to a 10 on bad days, but it's a four now, flaring up to a six on bad days, which is a huge improvement!'

Pain Management Pointers
Chronic Pain

Don't be deterred by chronic pain – it's just energy. According to Meta-Health master trainer Rob van Overbruggen,

> 'The one belief that can make pain excruciating is "I'm not taken care of" or "I'm alone." If someone is running this belief alongside the traumatic event that caused the pain then the body will start taking on a lot of water and causing extreme oedema (puffy hands/puffy face) and muscle and tendon pains will probably need morphine. When you resolve that belief, the body excretes more water and the pain reduces.'

Once you've built rapport with the client, you can ask whether they recognize that belief. If they do, you can work with this belief system straight away and see where it started by going back through the ECHO stream.

Client Homework

The essentials for pain management are:

1. Basic Tapping for Pain Management in between Sessions

Sometimes pain can be excruciating and present in the areas we use to tap, so use visuals to help find alternative methods such as imaginary golden hands coming in to tap on you, or by gently and slowly touching the points and taking deep breaths as you do so.

2. Keeping a Pain Journal

Ask clients to keep a journal and to note down their SUDS levels during the day, as well as any time the pain disappears. This can also help them realize that they're not always in pain. It can be tremendously enlightening to move from 'I'm always in terrible pain' to 'I'm in bad pain, worst in the mornings' etc. Most people suffering with chronic pain believe that it's a constant, but in actual fact there'll be times when it's less intense or goes away completely. This will also give you some clues to what might be triggering the pain.

Physical pain can be a factor driving people to try EFT and Matrix Reimprinting. If we can help these people manage their pain, it truly opens their minds to the possibilities of managing their own energy systems on a permanent basis. It's also an extremely rewarding area to work in, as the results can often be instantaneous, like flicking a switch. Tapping can become a person's painkillers.

A Diagnostic Approach to Pain

When we look into the fields of complex regional pain syndrome (CRPS) and phantom limb pain, it becomes very clear that the brain/mind is in charge of our pain signals. CRPS is a condition that baffles allopathic medicine. It's subtle, invisible and is often called the suicide disease. There is no bone damage or tissue damage, and often absolutely nothing physically wrong with the body. CRPS 'usually develops after an injury – which in most cases is a minor injury – but the pain experienced is out of all proportion to what you would normally expect'.[1] It can affect any part of the body and in terms of measuring the pain, people have rated it higher than childbirth.

Phantom limb pain is again significant. Remember that approximately 60 to 80 per cent of individuals with an amputation experience phantom sensations in their amputated limb, and the majority of the sensations are painful.[2] The brain is making the connection, the brain is tuning in to that limb's morphic field. Every body part has a virtual body part in the brain.

This is key in understanding how using a diagnostic approach to pain and disease can help us find the root cause, or root belief, of an illness.

This connection is nothing new. The power of the mind and how traumas affect certain areas of the body have been documented over the course of history in many cultures and traditions such as shamanism.

Louise Hay was one of the modern pioneers who intuitively knew that our attitudes to life and the language we used could cause specific ailments and pain in certain areas of our body.

Over the last 40 years, research carried out in several areas of science, such as embryology, neuroscience, epigenetics, anatomy, physiology and pathology, has brought forth much evidence that when a person experiences a shock, not only do they go into fight or flight mode, but the energy of the shock hits a specific part of the brain, corresponding to a particular organ. Indeed, the Meta-Health framework has compiled much empirical evidence and scientific data that show (through the use of MRI brain scans) the shock in the brain being linked with specific body parts.

The body then adapts to cope with that shock. This is meant to be a short-term adaptation, but pain and disease occur when we get stuck in the process.

These findings have taught us that our body doesn't make mistakes – it's always trying to gain resolution, and to adapt to a belief or perception.

It's important to note that the 'shock' is a matter of perception – it is the *belief* that is important.

Many of these areas of research, such as Meta-Health and German New Medicine, are complex systems that will take a considerable time to study, yet we want to simplify things here with regards to a diagnostic tool for pain management. So we're going to look at pain in the musculoskeletal system (bones, muscles, ligaments and joints), which is where 95 per cent of pain originates.

Pain as Part of the Healing Process

If we can move to a perception that pain is actually a sign of healing, we can find out where in the process we are and what trauma resolution we need to relieve it.

The Two Phases of Healing

There are several phases that the body goes through to heal itself, but here we are concerned with just two of them: the stress phase and the regeneration phase:

✧ In the stress phase, the body is under stress (which can be real or imagined) and adapts to cope with the situation.

✧ Following that there is the regeneration phase, which occurs when the person resolves the issue and the body moves into the healing process.

We go through these phases daily, perhaps without any problems. It's when the energy becomes stuck, unable to move through the phases or trapped in a cycle where it is being constantly retriggered, or the trauma is acute or prolonged, that the pain can become something that we need help to manage.

Imagine a bodybuilder working out at the gym. During his weightlifting session, he will lift more than he is comfortably able, with the clear intention of ripping and straining his muscles. This is the stress phase. It is important that he then rests this set of muscles so that they can repair in order to grow stronger than before. 'During the repair of the muscle, tissue swelling and oedema (fluid build-up) occur, all of which can cause pain and cramp until the muscle finally starts to return to normal.'[3] This is the regeneration phase and it is the point where the bodybuilder will feel the pain. After the regeneration phase, the muscle will be stronger and able to lift the same weight more easily than before.

This is the physical level of the two phases. There is also the psychological or 'belief' level. When the bodybuilder can't lift the weight, he will send the message to his muscles that he isn't strong enough to lift it, which signals to the muscles to go through the process of breakdown (stress) followed by regeneration to make them stronger for the future. They will be better able to cope the next time.

With regards to pain in the musculoskeletal system, the process is as follows:

1. First there needs to be the core belief 'I need to be strong in order to survive' – with which the majority of us can resonate.
2. Then there needs to be a shock, trauma or a trigger, a situation in which we didn't feel strong enough to survive. This can be real or a perceived threat.
3. Stress phase: The body then reacts to this situation in a specific area that feels the stress of 'not being strong enough', for example the thinning of the muscle resulting in a weakness.
4. Regeneration phase: This is where the body does feel strong enough and is moved into regeneration. With regards to muscles, the single fibres rupture and the body makes more liquid so that the muscles swell a little. It is in this phase that we experience pain in the area.

Clues in the Areas of the Body

As each part of the body has a dedicated function, if we look at the part of the body that the pain is in, we can begin to see what the message might be. Louise Hay also breaks down specific affirmations for certain organs and joints. For example, she quotes knee problems as 'Stubborn ego and pride. Fear. Inability to bend. Inflexibility. Won't give in.'[4]

The area of the body will give you some clues. What does that part of the body do? What makes that part of you hurt? If five people all fell over in exactly the same way, they would all get different injuries based on what organ or part of their body was in the stress phase and therefore weaker. A person who had concerns around responsibility might put their shoulder out, or perhaps an ankle if they were stressed about taking a step forwards in their life.

An accident is just an accident, but if we experience pain in an area, we can see there is a weakness there and therefore can ask questions about why it might be in the stress phase and what brought it into repair, or why it's the part of us that's experiencing pain. If we don't enter a repair phase and we remain under a high level of stress, that area will just get weaker and weaker until something happens to it.

Look at the skeleton and the snippets of case studies given below and you can see how the area of pain is related to the conflict and belief system. (We have taken these conflicts from the valuable Meta-Health research.)

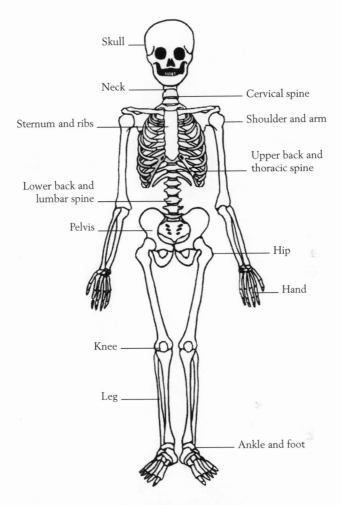

Skull

Neck

Sternum and ribs

Lower back and
lumbar spine

Pelvis

Knee

Leg

Cervical spine

Shoulder and arm

Upper back and
thoracic spine

Hip

Hand

Ankle and foot

The skeleton and areas of pain

Skull
Intellectual conflict

James suffered from pain at the top of his skull for many years. He was a schoolteacher, but felt he wasn't as qualified and knowledgeable as his colleagues. He always felt inadequate when the other teachers talked on subjects he was unsure about. This issue stemmed from a father who always put him down and called him stupid.

Neck and cervical spine
Moral self-devaluation conflict

Kia had recurring neck pain and believed that she was being treated unfairly at work and a colleague received a promotion over her.

Shoulder and arm
Parent/partner/child self-devaluation conflict

Sharon had experienced chronic pain in her shoulder for over 20 years. The issue was about 'shouldering the responsibility' for her ageing parents. She felt that she wasn't strong enough to cope.

Sternum and ribs
Male/female identity conflict

Mike had spent 20 years in military service. When he left the military, he had an identity crisis. This resulted in pain in his chest and ribs.

Upper back and thoracic spine
Central personality self-devaluation conflict

John believed his boss was being unfair to him when he continually accused him of shirking his responsibilities and not putting in the same hours as his colleagues. He never gave him any credit for his achievements either.

Lower back and lumbar spine
Central/core personality/personal balance

James was a 15-year-old who was shy and softly spoken. He felt that nobody ever listened to him either at school or at home. The more his friends and parents seemed to ignore him, the more he stopped trying to be heard.

Pelvis
Sexual devaluation conflict

Julia never felt able to satisfy her husband in bed, so she began to make excuses so she didn't have to have sex with him. She was, however, worried he'd look for sex elsewhere.

Hip
Inability to hold on or to withstand a situation

Florence was constantly struggling with needing to prove herself at work and never felt she was up to the job or deserved to be employed there.

Hand
Inability to grasp or let go of a person or situation

Maxine had chronic arthritis for 13 years as a result of one of her children being taken into care for over a week. She hadn't felt worthy enough or strong enough to hold on to her children.

Knee
Inability to kick or run away; can also be related to sports and flexibility conflicts

Jerome was a soccer player but hadn't played very well during one season and had often been left on the bench. This left him feeling that he wasn't 'strong enough' for the team. Soon he had a knee injury.

Leg
Conflict about being strong enough to get away

Gillian had bad leg pain and believed that she should have been able to run away from an attacker when she was a teenager.

Ankle and foot
Flexibility self-devaluation conflict

Simon was in a very stressful phase of his relationship. He felt trapped, that he wasn't strong enough to move forwards in any way. When his car broke down and he tried to push it forwards, he snapped the Achilles tendon in his ankle.

Diagnostic Questions

If you'd like to explore how you can use a root-cause diagnostic approach to pain, use the following questions to help pinpoint patterns and trigger points that can help you find the ECHO stream.

1. 'What does this part of the body do?'

Arms hold on to things, they pull things closer, perhaps to protect them, or they push things away. The more specifically you can identify the movement that causes the most pain, the easier it is to define the action and therefore what it is you aren't strong enough to do.

2. 'Do you relate to the idea that you don't feel strong enough?'
3. 'When did you feel strong enough or able to do something around the time that the pain started?'
4. 'What did you resolve that made you feel that you were strong enough?'

This is the 'sigh' moment, when things got better. But there's no energy in that moment, so what did that situation solve that was previously stressful for you? When you find that 'stressful' situation, go back and work with the ECHO from that time using the Classic Matrix Technique.

The beauty of working with a diagnostic approach and Matrix Reimprinting is that when we find the trauma that is specifically linked to a body part, or a resolved situation, we can easily find the relevant ECHO stream.

Meet Catherine, a sales representative who suffered with hip pain so that sleeping on one side was difficult and attending her Pilates class was painful. On the advice of her practitioner, she kept a pain journal and saw that the pain seemed to get worse after contact with members of her family.

Her practitioner knew that hip pain could be related to conflict about an inability to hold on or to withstand a situation. On gentle questioning about her family relationships, Catherine admitted she felt distant from her siblings, as they had all started their own family in the last few years and she was still single. She felt as if they had moved on and she hadn't.

This was the stress phase and every time Catherine had loving contact with her family it would feel resolved – the regeneration phase – hence she was stuck in this healing cycle.

She and her practitioner visited recent ECHOs that were related to this energy and belief, at a family christening and also at a time when Catherine's mother jokingly told her to 'Hurry up and get married and give me more grandkids!'

They traced the belief of 'having to keep up with my siblings' down the ECHO stream to a five-year-old ECHO watching her sister win a gold medal at gymnastics and feeling that she would never be in the same league. They tapped, released and resourced the ECHO so that she also won a medal and her sister reassured her that she was innately brilliant.

After the session, Catherine remarked that she had had no idea her hip pain could be related to this issue, but now she realized she'd been trying to compete with her sister all her life and had always felt unable to do so.

There were several other memories related to this belief and after using Matrix Reimprinting on this theme for a few more sessions, Catherine found her hip pain had completely gone.

Pain Relief for the Sporting Injury

There is understandably a lot of injury in this field, as first athletes are using their bodies more than most of us and second there is a lot of competition and pressure, which can compound the belief 'I'm not good enough' or 'I'm not strong enough.' Add those two components together and we can soon see how Matrix Reimprinting and a root-cause diagnostic approach can help athletes recover more quickly.

Tennis elbow is a great example of how the combination works. If a tennis player loses a match and this triggers 'I'm not strong enough' or 'I'm not flexible enough in my elbow', there is a perceived trauma, so the stress process becomes active and the muscles in the elbow begin to degenerate, get thinner. Then two or three weeks afterwards, the player suddenly wins and then feels 'I *am* strong enough.' This is when the elbow starts to restore itself through the process of oedema and this is when it hurts. It is when the player wins that the issue is resolved and the pain comes back. And it's when the cycle is retriggered through winning then losing that the process doesn't get resolved and the body's adaptation gets stuck. By using Matrix Reimprinting we can go back to the beginning of the belief 'I'm not strong enough' and move the ECHO through the process so the body can let go.

Medical Diagnosis

Matrix Reimprinting and Meta-Health practitioners work with the medical world, not against it. It is our dream that one day more doctors will join the many who are already using this technique.

If you or a client are experiencing chronic or recurring pain, it's advisable to get a full medical diagnosis. This is especially important if the pain isn't in the muscle or bone, as it will correspond to a different theme and belief.

For further reading on Meta-Health, we suggest the enlightening book *Meta Messages from Your Body* by Sam Thorpe.

Knowledge is…

Not power, at least not in this case. If you're asking questions of a client, you may well have an idea of what conflict might be running for them, but that's no excuse to tell them what might be going on for them. Using this information is about shining a light in the right place and inviting people in to see what they discover for themselves.

No Pain Blame

We can sometimes get confused about attracting events, pain or illness into our life. We can sit around and look for meaning in every scratch, fall or bruise, yet sometimes we just tumble. Remember we're never to blame and we're always doing the best we can with the information we have.

We will all be in pain at some point – that's inevitable. It's how quickly we can heal from it that counts.

If pain is the result of a single trauma rather than an ongoing cycle, it can clear astonishingly quickly. If there's no physiological damage, we can see quick shifts. Pain relief can be instantaneous, as when Gemma's CRPS went completely in one area of her body (as it was connected to one specific trauma and belief).

However, if there is nerve damage and degeneration of bones and/or tendons, it can take time for the body to repair itself. In terms of the body returning to a state of balance and flow, if the pendulum has been swung high in one way, it will need to swing equally high in the opposite direction to find its way back to equilibrium. If the pain has spread or is chronic, there can be many traumas to clear and time will be needed for the regeneration of the cells.

With Matrix Reimprinting and a diagnostic approach we can find new meaning in the old cliché 'No pain no gain.' When we experience pain or a disease in our body, we can find the 'gain' and use it to our advantage. We can find the trigger of that pain, why that part of our body is in a stress phase and find the belief and traumatic experience that have caused it. Pain is simply another way to find what core beliefs are present in our subconscious mind.

Chapter 11
RECOVERING FROM ABUSE

'Don't judge yourself from what others did to you.'
C. KENNEDY, OMORPHI

Abuse. A dirty word and one that we don't like to discuss. But it happens every day, in every town, in every country. It happens in our playgrounds, our workplaces, our hospitals and our family homes. It takes many forms, from the workplace bully who taunts a colleague to a father who sexually abuses his daughter, a mother who hits her son, a husband who beats his wife, a teacher who cruelly ridicules a student, a group of teenagers who write graffiti about a classmate. It may consist of a single act or repeated acts and it can occur in any kind of relationship. It affects all age groups and both genders.

The one thing all types of abuse have in common is that it leaves the victim feeling powerless and traumatized, so it's no surprise that we come across abuse in its many ugly guises in Matrix Reimprinting.

Beliefs from Abuse

Strong belief systems are formed as the result of abuse, as the victim will make the abusive trauma about themselves and attach a belief to it; a child who has been abused will often blame themselves rather than the perpetrator.

Clearing the trauma of abuse is so important for those who have experienced it in the first six years of life, because, as explained earlier, children are in a hypnogogic non-conscious state during this period and so these belief systems can be extremely damaging. This is also related to a child's development of boundaries: 'When inadequate safety boundary perception has not been developed in childhood, this usually leaves us with similar problems in adulthood.'[1]

There has been much research into the long-term physical, behavioural, societal and psychological impact on children who have been abused. Studies show that neglect and abuse can cause important regions of the brain to fail to form or grow properly, resulting in impaired development. These alterations in brain maturation have long-term consequences for cognitive, language and academic abilities and are also connected with mental health disorders.[2]

By working with ECHOs, we can work with the darkest abuse and safely keep the client dissociated. Remember, the ECHO holds the trauma of the abuse, locking it out of the conscious mind. We couldn't function if we lived in this traumatic state.

Abuse isn't an easy subject to talk about. Many talk therapies help the client become conscious of abuse, yet often people finish a course of therapy with their belief systems still in place.

Some of the common beliefs that appear with abuse are:

- ✧ 'I'm powerless.'
- ✧ 'I'm dirty.'
- ✧ 'I'm bad/naughty.'
- ✧ 'It was my fault.'
- ✧ 'I'm weak.'
- ✧ 'I didn't do anything about it.'
- ✧ 'It's not safe to confide in anyone.'
- ✧ 'I got special attention.'

✧ 'I got pleasure from it even though I knew it was wrong – I'm a bad person.'

If these aren't addressed and the energy around the trauma isn't released, then a person will continue to attract situations that prove that belief right. For example, if they believe they're a 'bad girl', they may go on to create situations that prove they are 'bad'.

Josie was 33 and had been working with a Matrix Reimprinting practitioner for a while via Skype, as she wanted some support after a divorce from a husband who'd been physically and emotionally abusive during their five-year marriage.

After using the ECHO to ECHO technique, they uncovered patterns of abuse and the belief 'It's always my fault', which Josie had carried throughout her life.

They traced it back to two pictures:

– Josie being about eight years old and being told off by her older sister and told that the 'situation' would be forgotten and not spoken about again.

– Josie being eight years old and her baby nephew lying on her tummy. Both of them were naked in a white room.

Josie had always suspected that there was abuse in her childhood, but hadn't been able to pinpoint who, where or what. Through gently exploring these pictures, she learned that her former brother-in-law (the father of her nephew) had abused both her and her nephew together and separately.

The eight-year-old ECHO was very defensive and didn't want to be touched or tapped on. Her dog helped to calm her down, but there were huge amounts of resentment and it was appropriate for her to go to a safe spot, which was a green lawn by the ocean with the sun shining and the dog by her side. At first the ECHO wanted to disappear into the water, but the practitioner gently guided her to feel safe and relaxed and agreed that she could stay there until the next session.

During the next session, they worked on all the feelings of worthlessness, guilt and shame held by this little ECHO and helped her feel good about herself.

In a following session they went through the emotional and physical abuse that Josie had been through with her ex-husband, and she remarked, 'I'd obviously chosen a partner who'd give me exactly the feelings that I'd dealt with all my life.'

In the Matrix, her ECHO took a picture of him, put it in a box and threw it into the ocean.

After that session Josie 'went for a run [and] cried a lot, but felt so much lighter and happier'.

As the dots connected from this deep belief, she began to see how it had affected every area of her life and relationships:

'During my teenage years, I always felt I was prey for men. I never got into relationships and found it hard to make male friends, as they always seemed to want more and said they'd fallen for me even though they were often in long-term relationships or married. I was always seen as a threat to their partners and I was told by many that it was my fault for being so happy, friendly and open-hearted.'

She told us:

'Dealing with these traumas helped me to find a trustworthy, caring partner such as I never thought to find. Now being able to look at these past experiences sometimes gives me goosebumps, but I'm proud of who I am today and have been able to help a few others who've had to deal with traumatic situations in their lives.'

When someone has been abused over a period of time, they're usually very aware of it and can spend their life going on a journey to heal from that experience. Yet sometimes the victim doesn't even realize that they're being abused. If they've grown up with a specific way of being, that behaviour is 'normal' and part of their accepted field of behaviour.

In Matrix Reimprinting, we don't deny that abuse happens, yet this technique is able to help the victim find peace and see the perpetrator in a different light. Resolving the trauma of an abusive situation brings such relief for the client, as often they've been carrying this burden around for years. Once we've released the trauma through tapping on the ECHO, new perceptions are able to come in. This is where the change happens: it's the transformation of the belief that was formed because of the situation. For example, Josie released the belief that it was always her fault, was able to see those experiences as something that happened and even 'felt proud' of who she was after going through them.

How to Work with Sexual Abuse
Pre-session Work for the Practitioner

The number one thing is not to prejudge. Even if you think that there may have been abuse in a client's past – perhaps your intuition is whispering to you or there is black energy present – it's not your role to mention the word 'abuse'. We only use the words that the client gives us. They may not be ready to go to that place. 'That place' might not even exist. Your role as a practitioner is to be as clear as possible, to get out of the way and hold the space for the client to go on their own journey through the Matrix, clearing the traumas that they're ready to face.

As abuse is such a taboo subject, it can be scary for new practitioners if a violent or sexual abusive memory comes up. If this resonates with you, it's time to do some clearing around your belief systems. The abuse, which may have become part of someone's story or identity, is not the trauma. Your job is to go and help the ECHO, that residue energy of the trauma, and help the client release it and form supportive beliefs going forwards.

> *Rosie was terrified that she'd been abused by her father, as she had high anxiety about remembering seeing her father's penis. She loved*

her father dearly, but had a lot of issues when it came to feeling safe in relationships and believed that it was 'not safe to be intimate'.

She and her practitioner did a lot of basic tapping to reduce the fears around what they might find and also reframed that they also might not find anything. They traced it back down to a five-year-old ECHO who'd walked in on her father having a bath. In the memory they both froze and her father shouted that she was a naughty girl. He was really angry and embarrassed.

Rosie tapped on her ECHO and her father so that a new perspective was brought in and they realized it was a simple mistake. Little Rosie realized that men and women had different bodies and it was OK, there was nothing to be scared of. They reimprinted a loving picture of her and her father having a cuddle and singing nursery rhymes.

Safety Check

Creating a safe strategy is always important, but is especially pertinent with abuse. We want the ECHO safe and OK to work with, or in a place of 'workability' – essentially, not frozen and unable to communicate with us.

Reread step 2 of the Classic Technique (*see page 73*).

Questions to ask are:

1. 'Who's in the room?'
2. 'Can we freeze the perpetrator?'
3. 'Do we need to take the ECHO out of the environment?'

Abreactions

If the client begins feeling the energy in a part of their body and associating with the ECHO, first use the safe technique that we outlined in Step 2 of the technique (*see page 73*). Ask them to step outside the ECHO and come into the memory slowly. Then follow with straight EFT and heart breathing if needed.

You may also find that the client is already tuning in to the next memory. Check in with them where they are and how their ECHO is looking, and this will tell you if they've already gone down the ECHO stream. If they've tuned in to the next memory, it's best to come out of it and finish the memory that you were working on.

Having said that, this really is a matter of intuition and judgement. For example, if you're working with a 15-year-old ECHO who is being bullied and then a 10-year-old ECHO comes up, you and the client can agree to clear that one first and come back to the 15-year-old ECHO later. Never be afraid of asking the client what they'd like to do: they always know best.

Make a mental note of who is in the room apart from the perpetrator and the victim, for example a sibling. When you've done the main work with the ECHO, you can refer back and ask, 'How's your sibling?' and find out if they need any tapping, as this can play an important role in the healing process.

Start at the End of the Traumatic Event

We always start at the end of an abusive trauma so that the client doesn't need to tell us about it or relive the details of what happened. We can pre-frame this work by telling the client that they can tell us as much or as little as they like, it's the *belief system* that we're searching for, what they made that trauma mean for them.

The other reason why we always start at the end of a traumatic event is that we don't want to deny that the abuse took place. For example, if we're resourcing an ECHO who has been abused, their first request is usually, 'I'd like this never to have happened,' which is where it becomes complicated, as it would be unethical to deny the abusive event. Instead, we can clear the energy, find the belief, transform it and move the ECHO safely through the trauma so that they're not left in the freeze, fight or flight response in the field.

How to Clear the Trauma: Workability

1. As per the Classic Technique, tap with the ECHO to release the freeze and trauma so that the ECHO is in a place of workability.

2. Keep going with the basic tapping technique until the ECHO feels OK and has released the response.

3. Refer back to the safety step and take them to a safe place to do this if you need to.

◆◆◆◆◆

Belief Resolution

Once you've tapped to release the trauma, you'll be questioning the ECHO to see what they made the abuse mean to them. As you know, it's from these realizations and beliefs that we help them find the right resources to transform and reimprint.

If the belief is about powerlessness, you could bring the perpetrator in so the ECHO stands up to them. You may also want to invite their higher self in and surrogately tap on them to understand why they acted as they did. Often this can lead to profound resolution, as they will have suffered abuse in their own past and this understanding can be very healing for a client, and often leads them to a place of forgiveness.

If an ECHO feels dirty, you may want to make some symbolic suggestions such as a cleansing waterfall, coloured light or angels to help them change that energy and allow them to emerge feeling lighter and cleaner.

Also, pay attention to where the energy is for the ECHO. For example, if it's in the throat, that gives you an indication that they aren't able to express themselves, so you could suggest that they might want to tell the perpetrator how it made them feel. This can be done through the ECHO or the client, as the ECHO may not feel able to do it, but having the older self do it is still empowering. It could be that they were never allowed to talk about it, so create a safe space where they can tell a family member or friend.

Another common belief is that they got attention from the abuse and they feel bad about this. Explain that they are just children and didn't understand that it was wrong; it doesn't make them bad. You could ask the client, 'From an adult perspective, is that belief true?' When they say, 'No,' ask them to give their ECHO all the reasons why it's not true. As soon as the client explains to the ECHO that they weren't at fault, there's a different story, a different perspective, a different belief for the ECHO and the client.

The Reimprinting Process

Once the ECHO has cleared the energy of the trauma and is feeling happy, and protected, ask questions to begin the reimprinting process. As always, make the reimprint relevant to the belief. How clean do they feel? How innocent do they feel? How safe do they feel right now?

The SUE scale works fantastically well here, as it will give an indication whether there's anything left to clear. For example, if the client gives a +5 on the picture, then you can ask: 'What would make the ECHO feel even better?' Use the ECHO's answers to discover the right resources for the situation. Even in the most terribly abusive situations the ECHO can get to a high positive and we can reimprint this feeling, belief and memory.

You may find that after imprinting a positive picture and then going back to revisit it, it may have gone down on the scale. This could be for two reasons: 1) that there are still some aspects to work on with this ECHO or 2) that neither you nor the client are ever going to truly feel positive about a past abusive situation. When working with a client, it may be that listening to their language is enough to know that they've moved on from it, they've had the conscious shift. Don't keep on at a client to reach a +10 if they're happy with the outcome.

As abuse has generally happened in the past, there's often no need to go to a future self, as reimprinting the past one will suffice. You may find that if there have been several abusive incidents, you'll need to clear many of these memories before the belief begins to shift in the present day.

Damien was in prison for being wrongly accused of sex-trafficking. His older brother had connections in Asia and had arranged for two Asian women to go over to Holland, as they wanted to work in the legal sex industry. Damien had married one of these women so that she could stay in the country legally. He had been arrested over this and sent to prison. His brother, however, was never imprisoned.

After working through the trauma of being sent to prison, Damien went down the ECHO stream to a 10-year-old ECHO who was being forced to give oral sex to an older boy to be part of the neighbourhood gang. This older boy controlled him and eventually they were caught, but Damien was blamed equally.

Damien and his practitioner worked on releasing all the shame and guilt he felt and uncovered the belief 'I'm always punished for sexual acts that are not my fault.' This was such a clear belief that he'd created it and looked for it all his life.

There had been several incidents to confirm that belief, such as a previous girlfriend accusing him of doing something sexual that he hadn't done. There was also an occasion when his friend's wife invited him over and his friend accused him of having sex with her.

There was a lot of clearing work for Damien to do around these traumas. However, seeing the common belief that connected them all gave him peace and a determination to transform this core belief.

Working with Other Types of Abuse

The word 'abuse' covers so many different situations, from workplace bullying to domestic violence. Under the umbrella of abuse there are big 'T' traumas and small 't' traumas. There's a huge difference between a playground squabble and sexual abuse or years of emotional abuse in an adult relationship.

As always, use the Classic Technique to create safety, release the trauma and find the belief.

Always start at the end of the memory to clear the trauma. However, with abusive memories that don't involve sexual abuse, it may be useful to change several aspects of the memory, for example the ECHO being able to stand up for themselves and reimprinting a feeling of strength. The belief will always give you an indicator of where to go next. Let the client be the guide.

Bullying

This is a common form of abuse and doesn't just happen in the playground but is found in the workplace and family home. It often comes from a person in authority, such as a manager or a work colleague, or even siblings. One of the Matrix trainers, Caroline Paulzen, commented, 'A lot of the clients coming to see me who are in their fifties or sixties are having problems with stress, anxiety and depression. I've often found that at some level this has come from bullying. It's so common.'

She went on to say, 'When somebody is being bullied in the workplace, if you go back down the ECHO stream, they've been bullied at school and possibly bullied at home... I can't remember a case where there wasn't some element of bullying in their past, be it from the home or the school. That then led into patterns of bullying in their adult life.'

This goes to show how important it is to address this global epidemic, which ranges from hounding by the media to the way we are parenting our children. (You can read more in Chapter 8 about how we can help release trauma as it's happening in our children's lives, before it creates traumatized ECHOs and damaging belief systems.)

Often beliefs around powerlessness, weakness and shame are prevalent with victims of bullying. Again, it's not about the trauma or the situation, it's the perception of the situation that matters. Workplace sniping, for example, might not bother some people, but for others it could cause extreme stress and anxiety.

Using the Movie Technique to test a bullying memory can be an efficient way to test whether an abuse memory is clear of trauma.

Recovering from Abuse

By using Matrix Reimprinting we can resolve the trauma of abuse and find the beliefs that were formed at that time. We often see huge shifts when working on single events of abuse, yet these are often the memories that we need to return to many times to uncover new lessons and beliefs.

It's never about denying that the abuse happened and it's always about finding peace. Resolving situations where we felt powerless, damaged and scared can be intensely healing. Time and time again, we've seen clients understand and forgive their perpetrators and learn from the situation. The victims aren't saying what the perpetrator did was right, but they're now able to let go of all that pain, anger and sadness.

The power of forgiveness isn't to be underestimated: 'There is a moment in our healing journey when our denial crumbles; we realize our experience and its continued effects on us won't "just go away". That's our breakthrough moment. It's the sun coming out to warm the seeds of hope so they can grow our personal garden of empowerment.'[3]

Chapter 12

TRANSFORMING GRIEF AND LOSS IN THE MATRIX

'Healing from grief is not the process of forgetting, it's the process of remembering with less pain and more joy.'

Anon

In the face of grief, many people feel completely helpless and believe that there is 'no way to get over it'. The morphic fields surrounding grief are so strong – family, cultural and universal fields that mesh together. Is it possible to find meaning and purpose in the death of a loved one? How can we ever recover from the loss of a child? Questions around grief can drop us into such depth of emotion. Yet in these depths there lies an opportunity for huge transformation and finding connection to something bigger than ourselves.

Matrix Reimprinting creates a space where we can connect with our deceased loved ones, a space where the unspoken becomes said, and forgiveness, energetic release and transformation are all possible. When we're traumatized, the ECHO that splits off seems to punch a hole into a different dimension. This dimension transcends time and space, so we're able to communicate not only with that ECHO, but all ECHOs from the past, present and future. We can reconnect with the spirits of people we've lost by working in this space.

On a course in Europe, Karl worked with Simone, whose seven-year-old son had died only a few months previously. The little boy had been physically and mentally disabled and during the course of his childhood Simone had lost everything, including her long-term relationship and career. The grief engulfing her was huge – she didn't know how to move through it and she felt guilty about any joy or laughter she found.

Through this sensitive work together, they went back to Simone's ECHO on the day that her son died. Simone tapped on her ECHO's shock and overwhelming emotions. They also tapped on her son's ECHO to release all his pain and fear about passing on.

Once as much of the trauma had been resolved as possible, Karl asked Simone if there was anywhere in the Matrix she would like to be with her son. She decided to sit underneath a beautiful oak tree in one of her favourite parks; her son was running around, both physically and mentally able. The one question that she wanted answered was: 'Why did my son have to go through such a tragic seven years?' She asked him that question and he said: 'I came down to teach you about love, Mummy. That's why I was here.'

At that moment Simone found resolution to her search for clarity about their situation. She and her son agreed that they could always come to this oak tree and be together in this happy place. Simone built up a picture of love, the greenness of the park and the cool wind on her face, and brought it through her body, sending it to every one of her cells and out through her heart.

After the session, there was still some remaining sadness, but the overwhelming grief was gone and Simone was massively comforted by the fact she now had a special place in the Matrix where she could be with her son.

Working with Death in the Matrix
Pre-framing in the First Session

Denying a death would be wrong. In Matrix Reimprinting we never deny anyone has died or bring them back to life in the Matrix. It's important to explain this when working with clients. Imagine if you hadn't pre-framed it with a client and you went to a trauma and asked what would they like to have happen and they said, 'For that person not to have died.' So, first of all, explain to them that what you will be able to do is help them with their overwhelming feelings and find out what that loss truly meant to them or what it made them believe about themselves.

When you've gained rapport with a client, you may want to teach them how to use the basic tapping sequence so that they can begin to manage their emotional reactions during the grieving process in between sessions.

Use some of these insightful questions to uncover their beliefs about death and find out where they are on their grieving journey and what resources and reframes to use.

✧ 'What do you feel has happened to your loved one?'

✧ 'What are your beliefs around death?'

✧ 'Is there anything you wish you had said or done with your loved one before they died?'

✧ 'Has anyone close to you died before?'

Clearing the Shock

Losing a loved one, whether it's expected or not, can be a shock to the system. As we know, when we have a shock it causes hundreds of chemical reactions in our body, not to mention the emotional, social and psychological impact. Working in the Matrix really helps this process, as it keeps us safely dissociated.

As always, clear the shock and trauma of the ECHO first.

Specific Aspects of Loss

After you've dealt with the shock of losing someone, tapping on that energy and letting it go, you can ask your client if there are any specific aspects of the death that they would like to address. Give them time and space to answer this.

> Meet Clara, a lady in her early thirties who'd lost her partner to cancer. There was one event during his illness that was troubling her immensely. She'd gone to visit him in hospital when he was very sick and had taken off her boots and put them beside his bed. A few minutes later, he'd got up and slipped over them. As he had already been very poorly, this fall had set him back physically.
>
> The guilt that Clara had around this aspect of his illness was enormous. With Matrix Reimprinting, however, she was able to go straight to that memory, communicate with her ECHO and clear the trauma and worry.
>
> Once she'd released all the guilt, she talked to her partner, who reassured her that he was OK and didn't hold her responsible in any way. So Clara was able to resolve 'the irresolvable' and move on from this aspect of her grief.

Communicating with the Deceased

As with surrogate work, when we bring family or friends into the memories, we can also bring in the deceased. Once you've cleared the shock and specific aspects of the loss, it's often an ideal time to bring the deceased person in.

In all the case studies we've read, in all the experience of the specialists we've talked to, whether the deceased was loved or hated by the person involved, their ECHO has always been their higher self. In this space, we can form an enduring connection with the deceased that can help greatly on the healing journey.

Sandra worked with Matrix practitioner Kathy Adams on her grief over the death of her son, Mark. Mark had been a brilliant doctor who, at the age of 40, had died suddenly in a road accident.

Sandra met Mark many times in the Matrix and as she felt new surges of grief at losing her child, she tapped on her ECHO to clear the energy. Mark would appear time and time again, infusing her heart with golden light. Towards the end of their work together, Sandra realized that she didn't want to let go of her grief totally because it would seem to her that she was abandoning Mark. In the morphic field there's a strong belief that it is impossible to be OK with the loss of a child.

On one particular occasion Sandra found herself standing under a beautiful waterfall with Mark. The water cleansed her of her remaining grief whilst Mark spoke to her. He told her that he wanted her to be free of the pain of grief and that although his body was no longer with her, he was very much there for her. He told her that her belief about not being able to be free of pain was not the truth. Then, as she stood there being cleansed by the waterfall, listening to Mark's words and feeling his love, he moved towards her and merged with her body, entering her heart.

When we find a space where we can communicate with our loved ones, we realize that death is not the end, that it is actually a joyful, expansive experience. We see true transformation in people's faces as the pain of grief lifts. The idea of forming an enduring connection with the deceased whilst embarking on a new life may seem an impossibility, yet Matrix Reimprinting makes it feel very real.

Meet Gilles, a French teacher whose daughter had committed suicide in her twenties. Despite it being over a decade since she'd died, he felt unable to forgive her for making that choice.

Through working with his ECHO in the Matrix and releasing the trauma when he'd found her body, he was able to release the shock from his field. He visibly shook when releasing this energy.

When his ECHO had let this go, he wanted to know why his daughter had decided to commit suicide. She came into the Matrix and talked with him at some length about her decision to die that day, explaining that it was part of her journey. This sensitive work was done in silence. Gilles understood her reasoning, was able to forgive her and found peace in her words.

Having found resolution, in the Matrix he went to his favourite place, a seafront, and his daughter joined him for long walks along the promenade. He found it very healing that he was able to access this new memory and talk to his daughter at any time.

Understanding Grief

What We Bring to Our Grief

None of us comes to grief with a blank sheet. We face it carrying all sorts of emotional baggage that we've gained in life, and grief can amplify those issues and beliefs. If we've had a previous loss that hasn't been dealt with in some way, if there are ECHOs that are stuck in the last cycle of grief, they'll be retriggered and compound the feelings of separation and loss.

Just like all the other subjects in this book, our beliefs and emotions about grief are completely individual, and are going to invoke an individual grieving experience. Some people get stuck in their grief and aren't able to move past it. There are also medical conditions, such as complicated grief and broken heart syndrome, that show us the scale of the grief spectrum. Often when we work with someone who's stuck in a painful cycle of grief they feel that they can't 'let go'. What are they trying to let go of? It can be so enlightening and helpful when they realize that it's not about letting go of the *person* but letting go of the *painful emotions*.

What evolves from this work is actually a new, often spiritual, closeness between the deceased and the person still here. It creates a new connection. When people let go of the pain of grief, they're left with the real person they knew and then they can appreciate the happy memories and know that the love that is present isn't going away.

Working on Our Own Grief

Just like all Matrix work, it's vital that practitioners stay out of the way when working with grief, death and loss. Because the morphic field around grief is so strong, it can tune people in very quickly, so if we haven't cleared our own traumas around grief, it could trigger us easily. If, however, we've worked through our own issues with regards to death and read some of the accounts of near-death experience, we'll truly be able to hold the space in an empathic, compassionate way. And our clients will feel our support. They will feel our strength and encouragement, which is so important in this work.

We advocate reading up on near-death experiences and also trying this swapping exercise.

Resolving the Unresolvable: Face-to-Face Swapping

This simple exercise will give you the opportunity to truly understand what we mean about communicating with our loved ones in the Matrix. It is a truly powerful exercise and it is also offers great practice in holding the space for another person.

1. Sit face to face with a swap partner. We'll call you the tapper and your partner the tappee.

2. The tappee chooses someone with whom they'd like to communicate who is no longer in their life, such as an old friend, an ex-partner or a parent. (They may be alive or dead.) They must also choose the point at which they will enter the Matrix. To enter the Matrix, you have to go via a point of trauma, as there's a huge difference between simply imagining

someone and working with them in the Matrix. So the entry point for the tappee could be the last time they saw them, when they died or a traumatic event where they were both present. It can be a resolved trauma, as the tappee is simply using the memory as an entry point.

3. Once the tappee has decided on the person and the point of entry, they close their eyes.

4. The tapper taps on all of their points in the basic sequence.

5. The tappee meets the person in the Matrix and communicates with them. They can say all the things they want to and resolve the unresolvable.

6. The tapper sits in silence, letting the tappee go at their own pace and letting them know that they are there if they need help at any point.

◆◆◆◆◆

It is also important to examine your own beliefs about death. What do you believe happens after life?

All the writings on near-death experience help us understand that dying is a process, that we're not alone but are looked after during this transition and that the essence or souls of those we love are ever-present. We can enable and empower our clients to create this reality for themselves.

Dr Peter Fenwick is Britain's leading clinical authority on near-death experiences and he brings together many people's stories in his book *The Art of Dying: What We Can Do to Achieve a Good Death*. When we're aware of some of these simple elements, we can use this knowledge to facilitate a good death experience in the Matrix. Recreating the wholesome death of a client's loved one can ease grief enormously.

Eleanor's husband, James, died of throat cancer and they had to endure many traumatic experiences of his tumour haemorrhaging. The doctor told them six months in advance of his death that this was how he was likely to die.

After James's death, Eleanor worked with her Matrix Reimprinting practitioner to go into the Matrix many times and soothe her ECHO's fears and resource herself and James as he bled. Her ECHO needed to know that it was OK for him to die. One of the ways in which they achieved peace around this was through Eleanor's beloved grandpa and James's parents and grandmother being present to reassure and help tap on their ECHOs.

One of the experiences that Eleanor created in the Matrix was a sense of love and joy remembered from previous times in her relationship with James. This was circulated around their bodies using pink light as she held, kissed and caressed James as he recovered from one of the traumatic bleeding experiences.

Following their work together, Eleanor told her practitioner, 'I'm in such a good space now. I feel James's comforting presence every day. In many different ways he feels always with me.' This was only nine months after his death.

Elisabeth Kübler-Ross wrote many books on death and dying and had her own near-death experience, which she called 'Cosmic Consciousness'. In this experience she merged into spiritual energy, the source of all light, where she vibrated alongside the whole planet, feeling great ecstasy and total love for everything – every leaf, every cloud, every blade of grass and every creature.

Anita Moorjani, whose near death from cancer led her to write the book *Dying to Be Me*, wrote that she felt awakened to the true magnificence of her soul, which was expanding beyond her body to include everything in the universe – every human, every animal, plant, insect, mountain, sea and inanimate object. She also felt love, joy, ecstasy and awe pour into her and engulf her.

Something else that those experiencing near death report is that we do not die alone. On our deathbed we are met by our deceased loved ones, who accompany us on our journey over the threshold of this life.

Grief in the Body

Unresolved trauma manifests in our body as pain or dis-ease. The trauma of losing someone is no different. There will always be a 'shock', whether that's finding out someone is terminally ill or finding someone dead. It will affect a specific part of the body, depending on what it means to us.

For example, if it's about separation, it will show up in skin problems; if it's a profound loss, it may affect the ovaries or testicles. As you'll see from Moira's account, it can affect the back, which is a core identity crisis.

> Moira was in her sixties when she first met her practitioner, Matrix trainer and grief specialist Janice Thompson, and she had had chronic back pain most of her adult life. In the first two sessions she could barely sit down it was so painful. At her initial session, she was apprehensive, as she'd been to see so many specialists by this point, and said: 'You're not going to open up a can of worms and leave me to deal with them again, as other people seem to do?' So during the first two sessions, they simply tapped on the pain in her back and got comfortable with each other.
>
> In the third session, Moira came in and said she'd like to talk about her baby brother, who'd died when she was around seven years old, and her mother, who'd blamed her for the death of the baby. They went into the Matrix, connected with Moira's seven-year-old ECHO and released the trauma of losing her brother and all the feelings that were attached to what her mother had said to her. The ECHO's belief was that she was no good, that it was all her fault.

As we've learned, lower back pain can be connected to issues around our core personality, essentially how we feel about ourselves. Moira hadn't felt good about herself since this event at the age of seven, and after this session, her back pain slowly began to get better. It had been chronic for a number of years, so there may have been some physical damage which would have taken time to heal, but overall, Moira felt a lot more in control and more optimistic about life. She also told Janice that the heavy feeling of depression she'd had all her life had lifted and she was starting to look forward to future events.

Hearts of Grief

Janice Thompson has developed a Hearts of Grief exercise to help with the different aspects of grief and empower people to work independently between Matrix Reimprinting sessions. Because grief can be all-encompassing, this simple process can help with gaining clarity, recognizing and owning our feelings, accepting where we are and realizing what we would like to move away from. Importantly, it also gives a sense of control, as grief can leave us feeling so powerless, lost and disconnected.

For the sake of ease we've simplified the exercise, yet to use this to full advantage, we suggest you download the larger body of work that is available as a Smartphone app (*see page 267 for more details*).

Exercise: Hearts of Grief

1. Choose eight of the most common negative emotions you've experienced since losing your loved one.

   If you haven't got eight, just list as many as you feel is right for you. (They don't have to be one word – they can be a whole sensation in a specific area of your body.) Some examples might be: anger, annoyance, anxiety, bitterness, confusion, depression, disgust, guilt, panic, paranoia, rage,

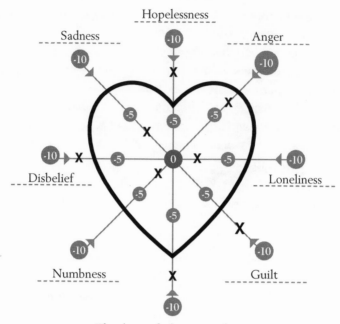

transformation to joy
www.janicethompson.co.uk
Janice Thompson MD

Hearts of grief

rejection, resentment, sadness…

2. Place one emotion on each of the points on the outer Heart of Grief as shown in the example above.

3. Give each an intensity rating, with 0 being 'no intensity at all' and –10 being 'extremely intense', and mark it with a cross. The more intense the feeling, the further out in the heart you mark the cross, and the less intense the feeling, the nearer to the centre you mark the cross.

4. As some homework in between sessions, you can tackle one area or one emotion at a time. Use tapping on each of the emotions and bring the intensity down so that you move nearer to the inner heart and a place of peace. For example, 'Even though I feel so drained from my grief, I love and accept myself anyway.'

5. Keep your results and repeat this exercise at regular intervals. As you work through your grief using Matrix Reimprinting you should find your negative emotions decreasing, and the Hearts of Grief is a great way to record your progress. Your scores will move nearer to the centre of the heart, towards a more neutral place of peace.

◆ ◆ ◆ ◆ ◆

Questions that practitioners can use alongside the Hearts of Grief are:

✧ 'Are any of these emotions really familiar to you? Were they familiar even before your loss?'

✧ 'Look at the emotion(s) you've scored as very intense [nearer the outer heart –10]. Do you know what's behind those feelings?'

✧ 'Do you have a specific feeling at any particular time of the day?'

✧ 'Do you have a specific feeling during a particular activity or situation?'

✧ 'What are you feeling right now? Is it on your heart of grief? Does it need to be?'

Losing someone hurts. The separation that we feel during the time of loss is like no other and we can instantly tune in to that huge morphic field of separation and grief. Bereavement can make us feel completely disconnected and in pain physically, spiritually and psychologically.

We'll all experience loss at some point in our life, and Matrix

Reimprinting offers an alternative to the pain and suffering of grief. Working with grief in the Matrix can become a profound, beautiful and healing experience. It reconnects us to our loved one and gives us the chance to see that death is not the end of our journey and that ultimately we are all one.

Chapter 13
CLEARING PHOBIAS AND ALLERGIES

'Fear makes the wolf bigger than he is.'

GERMAN PROVERB

What do allergies and phobias have in common and why have we grouped them together? How can hay fever and a spider phobia be related? Although it's not obvious at first thought, every phobic response or allergic reaction comes from a subconscious fear, a belief that something is dangerous and a threat to our survival. Remember that the body doesn't make mistakes, it simply adapts according to its perception of the situation and protects itself from danger.

When we're scared of something external (phobic), our body goes into fight or flight mode and wants to get as far away from the item as possible. When we have an internal bodily reaction (allergy), our body tries to rid itself of the substance. It's a hypersensitive reaction initiated by an immunological mechanism (IgE) – in other words, it's a defence mechanism. It's estimated by the World Health Organization that over 20 per cent of the world's population suffers from IgE-mediated allergic diseases, such as allergic asthma, allergic conjunctivitis, allergic rhinitis, anaphylaxis and atopic dermatitis/atopic eczema.[1]

Think about the milder allergic reactions such as runny eyes and nose – the body is trying to decontaminate itself from the substance, literally wash it out. Yet some people's bodies have adapted to the point where they can have a severe reaction known as anaphylactic shock, where symptoms include the swelling of the throat and mouth, severe asthma attacks and loss of consciousness, which can all be fatal. Here the body is closing itself off from the allergen – to the extent that it can actually kill itself!

So, how did we learn these responses? It can be through a variety of ways, but usually it's through a traumatic experience. If the subconscious attaches the cause of the trauma to an external object, we may end up with a phobia of that object, and if there's something in the body at the time of the trauma, it has the potential to become an allergy.

The other common ground that phobias and allergies share is that safety is paramount in this work, as the body is reacting in such an extreme way. They can also be fun to work with and satisfying to clear. In fact, resolving phobias has been one of the drivers of EFT's global success, as it's rather magical even to witness. Indeed, EFT works beautifully with phobias, yet what we've found with Matrix Reimprinting is that the work goes deeper, especially where beliefs are concerned. Every extreme reaction, whether it's a phobia or an allergy, is a golden opportunity to discover more about the belief blueprint that not only underpins our bodily reactions but also what we believe about ourselves and the world around us.

Also, there aren't many therapies that are able to locate where and how an allergy started. Within current health service structures there are no cures for allergies, only suppressants for the symptoms. As with all diseases, it's important to get to the root of the problem, which is what people can do for themselves using Matrix Reimprinting, tracing back through the ECHO stream to the core memory and how the belief and reaction started. As you'll see from the many case studies in this chapter, it's often impossible to guess where these reactions come from; it's only by doing the work with the ECHOs that you can pinpoint the specific events.

Phobias

We can create phobic responses in the same six ways that we create subconscious beliefs: conclusions based on a traumatic experience, modelling, a learning experience, post-hypnotic suggestion, teaching and repetition. Often a phobia involves more than one of these.

Fears make the transition into phobias when people have to change their life to avoid coming into contact with the thing that they fear.

Phobias are generally put into two groups; specific phobias (phobic responses to heights, small animals, dogs, etc.) and generalized phobias such as agoraphobia and social phobia.

Phobias and Fields

If a specific phobia has a relatively small field, with perhaps only one or two traumatic events underpinning it, it can be easy to clear, yet when there's a large field or a strong belief underpinning the reaction, it will take deeper work to get to the various levels. For example, a frog phobia may produce an extreme reaction, yet it's unlikely to have a huge field of behaviour around it, as people can avoid contact with frogs fairly easily. This will mean that there might only be a handful of frog-related ECHOs.

However, if someone has agoraphobia (fear of being in situations where escape may be difficult or help wouldn't be available if something went wrong), they'll have a large field of behaviour, with ECHOs and memories linked to it. This is because meeting people and going to new places are unavoidable.

Practitioners can pre-frame this with clients so that they understand that generalized phobias are likely to take longer to clear and may require more sessions and homework.

Questions for Phobias

When working with phobias, always ask the recipient if they can remember the first time that they had a phobic response and initially work with this memory. Once this is cleared, you can follow the ECHO stream to find earlier memories, ideally pre-six years of age.

If they can't remember the first time, use the Following the Energy method. This is an important technique when working with phobias. You can ask questions and imagine scenes about the phobia, but always be guided by the client. You don't need to take it too far (especially with severe phobias), just enough to access the energy so that there is something tangible to work on. For example, you could say, 'Imagine a spider running across the floor. How does that make you feel?'

As soon as there's energy present, ask the relevant questions and find the shape, colour and emotion. Once you have these, the next question will always be: 'When was the first time you felt this?' Once you have a memory, you can use the Classic Technique and then move through the ECHO stream, clearing the phobic response.

Phobias Can Be Fun

Once you've got to the core memory, as always, tap to release the energy that's stored there. Then, using the client's and ECHO's words, transform the ECHO's reaction to the phobia.

Give yourself and the client permission to do this in a fun way, as humour is often a great tonic and can result in cognitive shifts.

Meet Maria, who'd been scared of heights ever since she'd been rock climbing and had been abandoned on a rock face for quite some time before being rescued.

In her session, she revisited that ECHO and cleared the energy, and the ECHO asked to come down to the ground dressed as Mary Poppins with a magic umbrella. After one session, Maria's fear of heights was significantly reduced.

Dominique had been petrified of slugs ever since she'd seen a large number of them when she was young and living in Queensland, Australia. During her Matrix session, she grew these life-size slugs into a singing band with her ECHO being the lead singer and having a great time jiving with them all!

Safety and Testing Phobias

After resourcing the ECHO, don't send a new picture out into the field straight away. This step will come after you've tested the phobic reaction, which you do very slowly. With phobias there are so many levels that we can test on and it is always best to do this gradually, especially with severe phobias.

Testing the Phobia

1. Get the ECHO to test the phobia for you

When the ECHO has released all their original fears and is feeling positive, let them play with the object or situation that was causing the phobic response. For example, let them pick up a spider, fly a plane, stand at the top of a tall building, hold a snake, etc.

If there is still emotional intensity, tap on the ECHO and bring in new resources until they've released all the remaining energy. This will also give you a clue as to whether there are any related memories where the intensity needs to be cleared.

2. Get the client to test the phobia while they're in the Matrix

Ask the client to do exactly the same thing that the ECHO has just done, whilst in the Matrix. Run through the event with the client being tested. For example, if the ECHO is now fine with frogs, test that the client in the Matrix is too.

3. Test the phobia in the real world

Once the ECHO stream is completely clear of the phobic response, the final stage is testing the phobia in the real world through the use of words, pictures and, potentially, the real thing.

It's important to do that very slowly, especially with severe phobias. We would advise you to use evocative words first, then photos, before you attempt to bring in the actual object.

Once these stages are complete, you can reimprint the memory in the usual way. Although some reimprinted pictures can be fun and high on the SUE scale for the client, often they might be neutral, as it's more about the realization and understanding of where the reaction came from.

◆◆◆◆◆

The Beliefs Behind Phobias

Finding the beliefs behind phobic reactions is extremely rewarding and often results in deep realizations and cognitive shifts.

Remember Mo, who had the snake phobia? When Karl worked with him, the memory that presented itself was of a 13-year-old ECHO in the bath. A group of older boys had thrown a snake through the door which had landed in his bathwater. This ECHO was part of the filing system held in Mo's personal Matrix and despite trying lots of alternative therapies over the years, he hadn't been able to shift his snake phobia. This was because the snake had become symbolic of the situation and Mo's deeper belief at the time. This became apparent because Mo's ECHO remarked that he 'wasn't that bothered about the snake'. Yet the ECHO had an intense feeling of isolation and felt that he didn't belong. This stemmed from being bullied at boarding school and feeling confused and hurt as to why his father had sent him there in the first place.

As part of the resourcing process, Mo's father was brought into the picture and he and Mo had an intensely healing session in which his father's ECHO explained that he'd sent him away to school to protect him from Gaddafi, as the family was Libyan. From this conversation, both Mo and his ECHO understood that his father had sent him to boarding school out of love.

This new understanding was profoundly moving for Mo and soon he'd connected events throughout his life that had made him feel isolated and that he didn't belong.

Likewise, Linda was petrified of flying, yet it wasn't about the planes. When she tuned in to the energy, it went back to watching the events of 9/11 and from there it went down the ECHO stream to a six-year-old ECHO waiting at the window for her dad to bring her mum home from hospital. Yet when he came through the door, he was carrying her mum's belongings and said, 'Your mum is with the angels now. She won't be coming back.'

The connective belief was that people will die unexpectedly. That is what Linda made 9/11 mean for her and what flying meant for her. The events held the same energy as her mother dying unexpectedly when she was six years old.

So, deeper beliefs and meanings can be found when working with phobias and we can transform them so that we no longer have to be held to ransom by a phobic response. We can also see how a belief underpinning a phobia can filter out into the rest of our life.

Allergies

Globally, 200–250 million people may suffer from a food allergy,[2] with reactions varying from a swollen mouth to death. There's a difference between food sensitivities, the main culprits being dairy, wheat, gluten and caffeine, and a full-blown allergy, where the body's reactions take over. The most common allergies in the world today are related to food. Yet people are also allergic to dust, pet dander, mould and pollen, and there are rare cases of water, beer and even sunshine causing allergic reactions. Worldwide sensitization rates to one or more common allergens among schoolchildren are currently approaching 40–50 per cent,[3] which may be indicative of them developing more severe allergies later on in life.

We believe there are three main causes of allergies:

1. *Physiological:* A reduction in gut flora can cause food intolerances to substances such as dairy, wheat and gluten.

2. *Emotional:* The body may react to a substance it perceives as dangerous. This is the result of the substance being in the body, whether through the skin, through food or through inhalation, at the time of a perceived trauma.

3. *Generalized:* This means that numerous allergies from a range of external substances can build up simply by having core beliefs such as 'The world is a dangerous place.'

Physiological Allergies and Food Intolerances

There are certain foods that are not easily tolerated by the body, and our issues with them can increase with age. When we are young and have good immune and digestive systems with the right balance of enzymes and gut flora, we can eat foods that most nutritionists agree aren't good for us. Yet as we get older, we infiltrate our internal systems with substances and medications such as antibiotics, the contraceptive pill and alcohol, and these substances can destroy beneficial gut flora, leaving us unable to digest these foods easily and effectively, which may in turn lead to allergies.

When the natural gut flora is destroyed, we can also get 'leaky gut'. This term is often used to describe the process in which Candida burrows into the walls of the intestines and the partly digested food starts to leak into the bloodstream, at which point the white blood cells attack it, resulting in an uncomfortable 'allergic' reaction. Essentially, we can become sensitive to any food we eat a lot of.

This can be very common with auto-immune diseases such as fibromyalgia/ME and environmental illnesses where people can become hyper-allergic to everything in their surroundings. Although there will be a belief underpinning the auto-immune diseases, the physiological component does need to be addressed and we suggest that clients also get some nutritional support so that they can learn ways to rebuild their natural gut flora. Donna Gates's book, *The Body Ecology Diet: Recovering Your Health and Rebuilding Your Immunity* (Hay House, 2011), is an excellent guide for anyone looking for advice in this area.

Emotional Allergies

Emotional or trauma-based allergies are a result of having a substance in our body at the time something traumatic happens, so that the body associates that substance with trauma or stress and rejects it as dangerous.

Imagine it's Christmas day and a large table is filled with food. In the corner a young girl sits down amongst her family. Yet her mother is depressed and on this particular day she goes into the kitchen and cuts her wrists, resulting in a traumatic event for the child. From that point onwards, the young girl is allergic to every food she's eaten that day because of the trauma of the event.

With regard to emotional allergies, the subconscious mind has asked, 'What has caused this emotional reaction?' and concluded that it must be what's in the system. This can happen with any traumatic situation at any age, yet the belief that underpins it will have started pre-six.

Generalized Allergies

Allergies can become generalized, so that one individual can accumulate a whole collection of them. Sasha Allenby, the co-author of *Matrix*

Reimprinting Using EFT, had over 20 allergies when she started her journey with EFT and Matrix Reimprinting. In fact, when she went to train with Karl in EFT, she had to stay in a self-catering apartment with its own refrigeration rather than in residence with the other trainees, as she wouldn't have been able to attend had she not brought her own food.

It's important to recognize that there's often a crossover between the different types of allergy. For example, when Sasha used Matrix Reimprinting to transform the beliefs behind her ME/CFS, her symptoms improved, yet there was still nutritional work to be done to rebuild her immune system. Sasha now travels all over the world to deliver inspiring talks and workshops!

Beliefs behind Allergies

As with phobias, every allergic reaction that is based on trauma gives us an insight into a deeper belief that the client holds about themselves. Core events that underpin allergies can also be the start of a belief that filters out into the rest of their life. Resolving these can be a profound learning experience for both client and practitioner.

This happened when Karl worked with Kirsty. He often remarks he wishes he could have recorded this session, as it beautifully shows the stream of an intricate belief behind an allergic reaction.

> *Kirsty had suffered from hay fever for 10 years. Despite using EFT and Matrix Reimprinting to reduce her chronic symptoms, she still had major sneezing fits (sometimes up to 25 sneezes) and an uncomfortably itchy mouth for a couple of months of the year.*
>
> *Karl asked Kirsty to tune in to the energy of her symptoms and soon she was feeling tightness in her throat and desperation in her solar plexus. When asked to recall the first time she'd felt this energy, she described being in a park, aged 16, and having sexual relations with an older man 'just for the drugs'. This park was also the place where she'd truanted from school, smoked drugs for the first time at 12 years old and run to when she was in trouble at home during her teenage years.*

Karl went ECHO to ECHO and soon Kirsty had a memory of herself at 12, finding some cigarettes in a phone box. Her ECHO grabbed them and smoked them with some of the boys she was hanging around with at the time. This led to a memory of when she was around three years old and with a boy of the same age. As the memory unfolded, Kirsty explained that her three-year-old self was feeling bad, as she'd suggested to her friend that they urinate in the garden and use leaves to wipe themselves. Afterwards, the little ECHO had confessed to her mum what she'd done and her mum had scolded her and told her it was naughty. Little Kirsty then made this harmless event mean that she was a bad girl and made boys do bad things.

As they worked together to clear the energy around this event and had Mum telling the ECHO that she was a lovely good girl, Kirsty began connecting the dots. All her life she'd believed she was a 'bad girl' and that she led boys astray.

What was also fascinating was the theme of leaves running through the memories: 1) cannabis leaves; 2) tobacco leaves; 3) garden leaves. Kirsty remarked that she'd always felt disconnected from nature and scared of it in some way. It was one of those sessions that everyone in the room would remember, most of all Kirsty, because it highlighted her core belief, and Karl, because it showed how deep and intricate beliefs around allergies could be.

After the session, Kirsty cycled home with a friend and rolled around in some grass, deeply inhaling the earthy smells of nature. A year later she moved to the countryside with her family without so much as a sniffle.

Allergies and Fields

Like phobias, allergies can have very strong fields. What starts as a minor allergy can become more and more intense each time we have an allergic reaction, as the mind sends messages to the body that the substance is harmful, and the more times we have an allergic reaction, the stronger the field will become. Just take Kirsty's example of hay fever – every summer became a struggle because of the symptoms and she dreaded the months when it was at its worst. The field had become denser and filled with ECHOs who were feeling powerless against the onslaught of the allergen (which can also become generalized – grass, hay, pine, pollen, etc.). Add into the mix the family fields of behaviour and the idea that allergies are genetic, plus the cultural advertising of hay-fever drugs, and it's no wonder that it took some dedicated work to clear the final throes of this reaction.

Yet it's not always the case that allergies have very strong fields, and when we encounter an unusual allergy, one where the allergen can generally be avoided, it can be cleared in one session.

> *Meet Mia, who was allergic to avocados. Whilst living in Spain at the age of 20, she'd eaten an avocado salad and immediately thrown up, and from that day onwards she was allergic to them.*
>
> *As soon as she began to tap and tune in to the energy she felt nauseous and memories began to surface. The first ECHO, an infant, was locked in a cellar and couldn't get out. The next ECHO was running through woods being chased. The final ECHO was living on her own in Spain and feeling miserable, as she had no money and felt lonely and unsafe, and that was when she ate the avocado salad and vomited.*
>
> *What was the connection between the three? It was the feeling of not being safe: being locked in a cellar, being chased and being alone in a foreign country. Furthermore, the apartment Mia was living in when she'd eaten the salad was damp and musty – as was the cellar, as were the woods. The situation in Spain felt the same energetically as the woods and cellar. Mia's body attributed this to the avocado (the substance in her system) and believed it to be a threat to her survival. So she became allergic to avocados because they were linked to the belief that had formed pre-six: that she wasn't safe.*

First Steps in Allergies

✧ Ask the client how long they've had their allergy and if they've any idea what caused it. Has anyone else in their family got this allergy?

- If a client has multiple allergies, it's a good idea to ask them to separate out their symptoms so that you can begin work on one allergy at a time.

- If a client has an allergy that's indicative of the physical reduction of gut flora (IBS-type symptoms) then you can work with them to reduce the symptoms, but it's important to advocate the understanding of nutrition, so they can take steps to repair the damage. However, don't assume that it's just a 'gut flora' issue, as Karl found out with Amber when working with a milk allergy.

After initial questioning, Amber said that when she had milk she became light-headed and dizzy, which isn't a common reaction with dairy intolerance and is indicative of a trauma/emotional-based allergy.

Karl asked her to repeat 'I have this problem with milk' whilst slow tapping around her points. She immediately began to tune in to the energy – her breathing pattern changed and there was tightness in her chest. As she was associating with the ECHO and feeling the intensity of the energy, Karl asked her to do some heart breathing. She did so, opened her eyes and stood up to ground herself.

The first memory that arose was of her father standing over her cowering four-year-old ECHO and shouting. After removing him from the room for a few moments, Amber went and tapped on her ECHO, releasing the energy that she was feeling using conversational language such as 'All this tightness in your chest, all this fear of Daddy.' As soon as she'd released the energy, the ECHO stood upright and felt calmer.

The belief that Amber's ECHO had made that day was that the world wasn't safe and that Daddy didn't love her. Karl asked if there was any connection to milk, but at that point there wasn't.

Soon they were tapping on Dad and discovering that he was a sensitive man but the Second World War had left him devastated and with PTSD. After some tapping on him, the young ECHO was able to sit on his knee reading a book with him.

When they were looking at the picture, Amber gave it a +7 on the SUE scale, but to make it a little higher, she needed something to look forward to. They came up with a picture of her going to the local park and playing in the trees with her father. Both Amber and her ECHO felt elated at having something exciting to look forward to with her father. She brought through all the senses, emotions and colours of that picture and reimprinted it in the usual way.

When they tested the original picture, there was no emotional intensity left. Karl asked Amber to go back down the ECHO stream by asking the ECHO if there was anywhere else they could go where she had a problem with milk.

The next memory that came up was of a six-year-old ECHO who was about to start a new class at school. She was frozen with fear, as her new teacher was a tall, bearded man. After tapping to release the freeze, the ECHO said that she didn't like him, that his beard was dark and that it made her feel trapped.

Amber had a few quiet moments to herself regarding this 'trapped' realization, because she hadn't been allowed to go anywhere without her parents until she was 10 years old. This had instilled a belief that the world wasn't safe and that trying something new could be dangerous. Amber and her ECHO worked together to find the resources to help transform that belief, which centred around asking for help with her reading skills and receiving a school prize for being the 'most improved reader'.

As the connection to milk wasn't completely obvious, Karl questioned Amber (and her ECHO) about this and it emerged that Amber's mother was 'so overcaring that she got a job as the milk lady at the school'.

At this point, Mum came into the picture and the ECHO drank some milk in the Matrix and enjoyed it. As older Amber was feeling safe and secure, she also drank a bottle of milk in the Matrix. Several revelations later, she reimprinted a +10 picture.

At the end of the session, Karl tested Amber's reaction by asking her to imagine drinking a glass of milk. At the beginning of the session when *she'd been asked to tune in to the energy of milk, she had immediately felt emotional. This time, she exclaimed, 'I'd like some cheesecake now!'*

What's quite funny is that Amber e-mailed Karl a few months later and said that although she was pleased to be able to eat dairy again, she'd put on quite a bit of extra weight and was now tapping to reduce the urge to eat it!

Follow the Energy in Allergies

The majority of clients can't remember where their allergy began, which is why the Following the Energy technique works incredibly well here.

✧ Keep repeating back the symptoms whilst tapping on the client. This will tune them in to the energy of the reaction.

✧ Once they feel the energy, ask them where this goes back to. You can use a mixture of recall techniques such as Slow EFT and ECHO to ECHO to find the original memory of the allergy – this will be pre-six years of age.

✧ After the ECHO has tapped to release the intensity of the allergic reaction, create a new memory where the ECHO ingests or comes into contact with the allergen, which no longer causes a reaction.

Testing Allergies

Like phobias, it's important to test the allergy in a safe environment. Ideally, you will want the ECHO to enjoy being with the allergen, for example, stroking a dog when they've previously been allergic to the dog hair or eating the food to which they had the allergy.

✧ Test the ECHO's reaction to the allergy first and then gradually introduce the allergen back to the client through words, pictures and imagination. For example, if someone is allergic to oranges and you want to test the allergy, ask them to imagine oranges on a plate and how that makes them feel.

✧ Then move it on to where they imagine picking up an orange and eating it. Their reaction will give you a clue as to whether there's still energy left to clear. If so, they can tune in to it and find the relevant ECHO or go back into the core memory and find the remaining aspect.

✧ If the reaction is clear in the imagination, we suggest you test the allergic reaction as it occurs in life rather than go specifically looking for it.

Safety with Allergies

For some people, their body has adapted to their allergen to the point where contact with it can be fatal. Remember that the subconscious mind cannot decipher between real or imagined situations, so if you are asking a client to tune in to the energy of the allergic reaction it can be dangerous. Therefore, only work with experienced practitioners who will ensure that they have the correct drugs and equipment, such as an adrenaline auto-injector, present during the sessions.

Clearing allergies with Matrix Reimprinting can be a rewarding experience and is also a good subject for group demonstrations. Within many health services, allergy testing is available, yet the resulting advice is usually a variation of 'Avoid exposure to the substance.' With Matrix Reimprinting, it's possible to trace back the trigger of an allergic reaction in one session. And, even better, it's possible to clear it too.

Chapter 14

LOVING OUR BODY IMAGE

'To lose confidence in one's body is to lose confidence in oneself.'

SIMONE DE BEAUVOIR

Do you love the way you look in the mirror? Do you like your face but not your tummy, arms or bottom? Are you too fat, too thin? Do you have great hair? A symmetrical face? Good teeth? Do you like the colour of your skin?

Most of us have an awareness of our body image – how we present ourselves to the world. There are parts we like and parts of which we aren't so fond. Some people detest the way they look and can't bear to gaze in the mirror, while others scrutinize their appearance and are always on the lookout for their 'faults'.

What about the images to which we're subjected by the media on a daily basis? The sexualization of women, the perfect body dimensions, a toned physique and don't even mention airbrushing! We're bombarded with messages about body image every single day. So it's hardly surprising that most bookstores have a maze of self-help books proclaiming they have the answer to achieving the perfect body, whether through beauty treatments, exercise routines or diet. With this constant bombardment both from our internal head-chatter and the media, it can take systematic work to address the fields of belief surrounding our body image. The neural pathways containing the information are deeply ingrained and are mirrored to us on a daily, often an hourly, basis.

Our body image will always be the result of our core beliefs. So, working with it is one way down the ECHO stream to find that source of the belief that may be causing a whole river of negativity. There can also be a crossover with addictive behaviour, as if we don't have a high regard for our body we may 'abuse' it, knowingly or unknowingly, through various addictions such as food, drugs, alcohol, sex and self-harm, as a way of managing our reality. But it's never about the food, or the substance we might be using. It's always the beliefs and traumatic events we've been through that are underneath the physical and mental reactions we have about our body image.

There's no set protocol for working with body image, as under this umbrella term there will be behaviour that will need addressing as well as beliefs. In order to uncover that behaviour and those beliefs, as well as offer tools to ensure the best chance of success, we've split this chapter into three sections:

1. Awareness of body-image perception.
2. The Classic Technique for body-image transformation.
3. Building a healthy body image.

Remember, knowing the theory won't change anything – it's questioning, tapping and commitment that will bring about the real change in this work.

Awareness of Body-Image Perception

The first step is to become aware of what we're saying to ourselves about our body. There is often a lot of 'story' with body image and it's key to use insightful questions to find out what's really going on.

Insightful Questions to Ask

✧ 'What do you believe about your body image/size and shape?'

✧ 'When did you first start to believe these things?'

✧ 'What experiences from the past do you think contribute to how you feel/think about yourself?'

✧ 'Are these beliefs your own beliefs? Or were they handed down to you?' (Family saying, 'We've always been big,' for example, or hearing it said that 'Men only like women who are...')

✧ 'What parts of your body don't you like?' (*Use a body outline; see page 229.*)

✧ What parts of your body do you like?' (*Use a body outline; see page 229.*)

✧ 'Do you have any worries, concerns or fears about having a healthy body image and confidence in your shape?'

✧ 'What will you stop doing once your beliefs about your body image have changed?'

✧ 'What will you start doing?'

✧ 'How will changing your body image affect those around you?' (Jealous friends, insecure family members, possessive partner...)

To find associations around food, ask:

✧ 'What would you say was your "comfort food"?'

✧ 'Was food ever given/withheld as a reward/punishment in your life?'

✧ 'When are you most likely to eat outside planned mealtimes – e.g., when you are bored, lonely, upset, tired?'

Ask well as asking these questions, you can:

✧ Listen for key words: 'fat', 'ugly', 'rejected', 'unloved', 'plain', 'old', 'skinny', 'short', 'tall'.

✧ Listen for jokes that a client might make about themselves or derogatory names for certain body parts.

♦ When working with a client, ask them to rate how much they love the way they look out of 100 per cent. This will give you a starting point for your sessions together.

Using the Classic Technique for Body-Image Transformation

Once you have an idea of what the mind-chatter is saying to you or your client, you can use the Classic Technique to connect with the ECHOs.

As we mentioned earlier, there's no set protocol for working with body image. It's a case of starting with one aspect, one body part or one belief. You'll have lots of information from the questions above. We suggest that you go to the answers that bring up the most emotion and follow those ECHO streams first.

Meet Tony, a black British manager who was having a terrible time as he thought the colour of his skin was causing him problems with his staff.

With his practitioner, Tony explored his past to find when he'd felt this way before. Through the ECHO stream they traced it back to times when he'd been bullied as a child because he was the only black boy in his class. Through this process, Tony realized that he was projecting his own belief of not being accepted or respected because of the colour of his skin onto his current situation.

Working with his practitioner and using a combination of Matrix Reimprinting and practical exercises, he was able to reimprint the memories of being bullied with scenes where he felt accepted. This in turn made him feel more effective as a manager, he became more assertive and confident in his delivery to his team and in one-to-one meetings with his staff. He enjoyed some huge personal achievements at work and the dynamic of his whole team changed. In the process, he gained new proof that his skin colour hadn't limited him at all – it was only his old beliefs and fears.

As always, the ECHOs hold the key. As soon as memories surface such as 'That time I was called fat by the other kids' or 'I had to wear braces when I was 13' then you have a memory on which you can use the Classic Technique. Follow this to the core beliefs by using the ECHO to ECHO Technique, so that the origin of the belief is cleared.

When we've a deeply ingrained belief about our body, there'll be several events that feel connected. As we're aware, when a belief is formed, it can 'play out' by 'attracting' more of the same unwanted events (because we believe it will happen, it does happen, or we behave in ways that attract more of the same experiences to us). When working with clients, we must be very careful how we word this so as not to 'blame' them. Instead, ask how having this belief has impacted their life both positively (for secondary gain) and negatively (so that we can relate to how the beliefs have formed patterns in life).

Meet Angela, who after several Matrix Reimprinting sessions realized that she used her extra weight as protection. She'd been raped and forced to engage in other unwanted sexual acts in her teens and had later been raped whilst on a date, and she believed that the way she looked had attracted these unwanted experiences to her. She also felt flawed, dirty and guilty. She was big-busted and thought that this was the focus of sexual attention, so she would cover herself up and not reveal any cleavage when out socially or on holiday for fear of the past repeating itself. She desperately wanted to be in a loving relationship, but the fear of being raped by possible suitors on dates felt too big to overcome.

With her practitioner, Angela explored these events and went into the Matrix and tapped on family members who had unwittingly put her in risky situations. This uncovered the core belief 'I have to go along with things that other people want and can only attract negative sexual experiences.'

In working through the contributing memories underpinning this belief (predominately the sexual experiences) and revisiting each memory several times, Angela began to love her body and within a year she was in a loving relationship.

From then on, her whole life changed: she moved house and found work that was fulfilling and her health and general wellbeing also improved.

It can take sustained work to clear beliefs around body image. If someone has believed that they're 'fat' or 'ugly' for 30 years and silently said it to themselves every time they've looked in the mirror, then one hour of Matrix Reimprinting isn't going to eradicate that completely. The reason we've given so many insightful questions is that you may wish to continue exploring internal and external references of self-hatred and self-loathing.

It's important to let the client set the goal for their own therapy. It's not a therapist's job to second-guess what their client wants to achieve, so ensuring this is clarified right at the beginning of therapy is imperative. Therapy is a process, whether it involves a single session or numerous sessions spread over a period of time. As such it is also the responsibility of the therapist to reassess at different stages how the work is progressing and determine if the original goal has been achieved, or if a new goal needs to be set. This is especially relevant in body image, as the goalposts may continually change.

However, once the core beliefs have been discovered and transformed into supportive beliefs, such as 'I'm good-looking' or 'I like the way I look' or even the most obvious one from the EFT set-up statement, 'I love and accept myself anyway', deep change has begun. Huge shifts can happen in single sessions and as body-image specialist Wendy Fry, author of *Find You, Find Love*, says, 'Many clients enjoy this technique and laugh at what they're creating to change the meanings and perceptions they placed on past experiences. It gives clients such freedom to be able to do or say what they didn't do or say at the time. They literally have free rein over their thoughts and actions inside the Matrix and this is such an amazing experience to have.'

Testing, Beliefs and the Meta Perspective

Like all Matrix Reimprinting work, testing is crucial. So continue checking in with the ECHOs to hear their perceptions of their body image. What else needs changing? Why do they feel the way they do?

Meet Margaret, who really wanted to lose weight and was eating sensibly, had set herself goals and even hired a personal trainer. Yet she was still unable to lose the excess two stone that she was carrying and often self-sabotaged her progress with sugary treats.

When she worked with her Matrix Reimprinting practitioner, she connected with her ECHO, whose mother was 'angry and thin', yet her next-door neighbour was a large lady who was rich, always had a smile on her face, had an expensive car and often gave the ECHO nice treats.

Margaret often turned to this neighbour when she was feeling down and saw her as an angel-type figure in her life. Her ECHO had therefore associated being fat with being lovely, happy and rich, and being thin with being mean and angry.

Margaret had an internal conflict and her subconscious mind was protecting her from becoming thin and therefore 'angry and miserable'. Through working in the Matrix, she was able to transform this belief by speaking to the neighbour and her mother about her concerns. They reassured her that their outlook on life had nothing to do with their size – it was simply their current situation.

It was through connecting the dots of this belief that Margaret was able to see her relationship with food differently and eat in a much more conscious way.

Pre-frame with your clients that it's likely that you'll revisit core memories at least twice to see what new insights can be discovered. As you will have used the questions to establish what type of beliefs are present, keep checking back in with these to see what has shifted.

Core Beliefs

You may also uncover beliefs around exercise and dieting that need addressing. As Nick Ortner, author of *The Tapping Solution*, aptly states, 'I wish I could say that tapping will make any food you eat healthier. But even with an elevated consciousness, positive thoughts and a high vibration, you can't turn that McDonald's cheeseburger into something nourishing for your body!'[1]

There's a huge difference between believing that you're overweight and unlovable and being overweight and feeling OK about it, knowing that you're still a beautiful human being worthy of love and affection. If a client desires to lose weight, it is important that you also discuss the use of goals, both to help them and so that they can measure their success and identify triggers along the way.

Working with the physical self is also a gradual process. If someone has issues with their body weight and would like to lose two stone, then you could use the ideas in Chapter 15 to aid the process.

Messages from the Body

We also can't ignore the messages from the body if there's a physical ailment present and that is the body-image 'issue' that the client is struggling with. What might a bodily symptom mean for the client (*see page 156*)? For example, skin issues such as acne, eczema or psoriasis – where is it on the body? What might that condition be keeping the person safe from? Remember it's never about the 'issue' and always about how the client feels about it and what they believe to be true for them.

Building a Positive Body Image

Three is the magic number in this chapter, as we also see this working most effectively if we use a three-pronged approach:

1. Managing the mind-chatter (cravings/ negativity) using basic EFT.

2.   Positive Field Imprinting.

3.   Practical exercises to aid success with the body image.

Once you've cleared out the old fields of behaviour around body image, there are numerous ways in which you can build a positive body-image imprint, either for yourself or for a client. When working with a client, be guided by them and how much 'homeplay' they're willing to undertake.

Acceptance is the point here. It might be that a client feels strong enough to embark on a new exercise routine, diet or shopping spree to help them feel happier and healthier. Yet it might also mean that they decide to have breast implants! It's not our place as practitioners to judge the right way for someone to feel great about their body. Just as we can't guess where beliefs stem from, so we can't guess what someone's ideal body image is. The answers come from within, not from our advice.

Basic EFT

To start with, use basic EFT to manage the mind-chatter. This can be used to counter negative affirmations or cravings for substances that you know will harm the body, or even to start their day on the right foot. It can also be an effective tool for standing in front of the mirror and listening to your thoughts about your body. Just five minutes' tapping a day can help clear negative emotions we have about our bodies.

When working with clients, teach them basic EFT. It also shows them they can take their healing into their own hands. Always remind them that they can just use the finger points if they feel self-conscious about doing full rounds in public.

Positive Field Imprinting

The next phase is imprinting positive beliefs into the field.

Positive Belief Imprinting

Step 1: A Future Self

Once the ECHO is trauma-free and has resolution, ask them to go to a picture of a future self where the original issue has been resolved and there's a new picture of success. With regards to the body, this could mean that the ECHO is happy with their dress size, skin tone, fitness level, etc. The future self should feel completely safe and connected.

Ask yourself, or your client, 'How does it feel looking at yourself in that body?'

Elicit the same sensory information as in the reimprinting process by asking open questions relevant to the subject of body image:

1. 'What are you wearing?'

2. 'What are people saying about your appearance?'

3. 'How does your ECHO feel in their body?'

4. 'What part of their body do they really like?'

When you're creating a future body image for the first time, doubt can creep in, as you may not quite believe you can look like that. As a practitioner, you have a few choices:

✧ Go back and clear the aspects that remain.

✧ Do some basic EFT to remove some of the doubt.

✧ 'Create it until you make it.'

This means that although the picture isn't 100 per cent clear, sometimes we have to work with what we've got. The more often we focus on the positive picture, however, the easier it will become. This can be a vital tool when time is running out in a session with a client and we want to end with a positive picture for them to use in their homeplay.

Step 2: Associating with the Future ECHO

Step into/ask the client to step into the future self and feel all that energy that they feel – all that safety, joy, connection and love for their own body.

Step 3: Reimprinting Process

Before you reimprint this picture in the usual way, you can also ask the future self if they have any guidance with regards to how they feel about their body. This is sensitive work, so when working with a client, let them tell you if they wish to share their findings.

Build this positive picture to a high number on the SUE scale and reimprint in the normal way.

When working with a client, you could record this process via their Smartphone so that they have it ready for the next step.

Step 4: The 21-Day Process

You will need to make a note of that picture and reimprint it for 21 days. Here are the instructions for a client to take home with them for this process:

1. Spend three to five minutes in the morning shortly after waking and in the evening before going to sleep reimprinting your new memory.

2. Close your eyes and reconnect to the new memory with all your senses.

3. Follow the reimprinting process as above so that the new memory and vibration are sent to all your cells.

◆◆◆◆◆

Homeplay

Here are some practical exercises for a new Body-Image Field Imprint that you can try at home:

Write Apology and Thank-you Letters

1. Write two letters, the first one apologizing to your body for all the nasty, hateful and unloving things you've said to it over the years (allow yourself to express your emotions freely).

2. Use the basic tapping protocol as you read this out loud to yourself.

3. Then write a thank-you letter to your body for how it has kept you breathing, functioning, talking and walking, etc., for all these years. Add in all the new changes you're working on and write the letter in the present tense as if you're already in this position. Be thankful for this new version of yourself.

◆◆◆◆◆

Use Mirror Work

Using a mirror can be intensely powerful when connecting to your inner dialogue. Louise Hay has been a huge advocate of using mirrors to increase self-love.

1. At least once a day – in fact, every time you look in the mirror – say to yourself: 'I love you, [insert name], I really love you.'

2. For many people this will bring stuff up, which is great! This is what this work is for, to bring that 'stuff' up, those emotions, those barriers that have stopped us loving ourselves just as we are. What do we want to do when we bring stuff up? Yes, tap on it, chase the energy and find the relevant ECHOs.

3. Continue this exercise for at least 30 days and watch what happens!

♦♦♦♦♦

Create a Body Outline

1. What parts of your body do you like? What parts of your body don't you like?

2. Draw a basic outline of a body and mark down your ideas, thoughts and feelings on the specific body parts that you do and don't like.

3. Then use basic EFT to manage the negative mind-chatter about those parts. This will help you to understand your language patterns about your body. It will also help the memories to rise to the surface.

4. When they do, go in and connect with the ECHOs so that you can use the Classic Technique to imprint supportive new beliefs.

♦♦♦♦♦

Practise Mutual Complimenting

This is perfect to do with a swap partner.

1. Get together for 10 minutes with your swap partner or another person you like and trust. Set a timer for five minutes or note the time on a watch or clock.

2. One of you compliments the other for five minutes.

3. Then you swap over.

4. Notice how you feel about yourself after the exercise. How does receiving compliments make you feel?

You can use this exercise to tune in to the energy and find the ECHOs who need to hear these words about themselves.

◆◆◆◆◆

When we transform our beliefs about our body image, we transform how we are perceived in the world. The beautiful thing about using Matrix Reimprinting for this is that we can go back to the times when our beliefs were formed and change them.

We're not 'broken' or 'imperfect' people – that's just our perceptions about ourselves being translated into our body image. If we consistently tell ourselves that we're too fat, too thin, have the wrong shape, the wrong look, who are we comparing ourselves to anyway? Magazine images of 'perfection' are a fantasy, and many models and celebrities are themselves wracked with insecurity and lack of confidence, despite their cleverly manipulated public image.

Many of us are so fixated on the physical way that we appear in this reality that often we need to work with this first. But in learning to accept our body image, we open ourselves up to new ways of thinking about ourselves.

If we can look into a mirror and tell ourselves that we truly love the person looking back at us, well, our world will have changed.

Chapter 15

ACHIEVING OUR GOALS

'While intent is the seed of manifestation, action is the water that nourishes the seed. Your actions must reflect your goals in order to achieve true success.'

STEVE MARABOLI

What is it you really want to achieve in this lifetime? Inner peace? Financial freedom? Deep romantic love? To travel the world? Write a book? Perhaps all of the above?

If we live a life we love, we're happier, live longer and have better health and relationships. It's simple when we put it like that – after all, who wants to be miserable? And if we aren't living a life we love, chances are we're being stressed out by it, and we know what stress does…

If we can treat ourselves and our clients holistically, with a view to discovering where we want to get to, rather than where we want to get away from, then we're visualizing (and moving towards) lives that are full of joy, abundance, vitality and freedom. But how do we know what we want without taking time to think, plan and take inspired action? Setting goals is the answer.

When we set goals, we're making our intentions clear and sending out a vibrational frequency that we hope will be met. If we can align ourselves both consciously and subconsciously with that frequency, we'll have faster, greater success.

Meet Jayne, who wants a new romantic relationship in her life. She's using all the popular techniques such as gratitude, affirmations and visualizations, yet she has still not met her soul mate. She's taking inspired action like going on blind dates and doing speed dating and internet dating, but feels she is attracting the 'wrong' type of guy.

Despite all the conscious self-work Jayne is undertaking, in her subconscious drawer marked 'relationships' are all the ECHOs who have been hurt before and who are carrying past rejections and believe that relationships are dangerous. They are energetically keeping Jayne away from a situation where she could get hurt again. Her conscious intention is being blocked by the beliefs in her subconscious.

◆◆◆◆◆

What about Michael, who wants to earn £30K through his coaching practice? He's done his business plan and he's got great links through his local chamber of commerce and some fantastic testimonials. He knows he needs 10 clients a week, but he never seems to get more than six.

In his subconscious drawer are a host of beliefs around being successful. His ECHOs are afraid of earning more than his parents and attracting jealousy from his siblings.

If our plans just aren't happening, it is our subconscious beliefs that need addressing. That's not to say that other techniques, such as affirmations, don't work – eventually they will – but the way to seriously move our goals forwards is by doing the inner work with Matrix Reimprinting.

On the flipside, when we do transform our beliefs into a supportive platform for our life, then using affirmations and visualizations, including dreamboards, will boost our manifestation prowess – not to mention they're a rather fun pastime!

Our Goals, Our Beliefs

Under 5 per cent of the population set goals, despite it being an acknowledged strategy to achieve success. Some of the reasons why are fear of failure, fear of success, the time and effort involved and not knowing how, as it's not a skill most of us have ever been taught.

This is where Matrix Reimprinting helps us and our clients explore the beliefs and self-sabotaging whispers that might be holding us back from achieving our goals.

Setting Goals

We invite you to look at your goals and explore the beliefs that are underpinning them. Grab yourself a piece of paper and write down 30 things you'd like to achieve in your lifetime. Here are some of the common areas that you may want to set goals in:

✧ family

✧ relationships

✧ home and environment

✧ leisure and fun time

✧ spirituality

✧ health

✧ money

✧ work and career

✧ socializing

✧ creativity

This exercise is a way to get your goal-setting creativity flowing. It's also a great exercise to give clients before their first session.

It gives an idea of their dreams and aspirations and can also help with suggestions for ECHOs and the reimprinting process during the session, especially when it comes to working with a future self.

Your goals can be big, joyful, specific, vague or so huge that they seem completely unattainable from where you're sitting right now.

Soon, you'll have a long list of goals and simply looking at them might cause you to feel overwhelmed. If this is the case for you, use basic tapping to bring that feeling down.

In his bestselling book *The Seven Habits of Highly Effective People*, Stephen Covey states that the one thing 'all successful men have in common is putting important things first'. Caryl Westmore, in her book *Goal Success*, elaborates by asking, 'What one goal – if you were to accomplish it this coming year – would have the greatest positive impact on your other goals and your life?'

◆◆◆◆◆

'Once you have your answer, this becomes your "Golden Goal",' says Caryl, who has developed this term in her protocol Matrix Goals Reimprinting, where she helps clients to achieve their dreams and goals and live the life they love.

Working with a Golden Goal

When working with a specific goal, whether it's to visit Paris or own a dog, the first question should always be: 'Why do I want to achieve this?'

It's never about having a holiday, it's about what that trip means for you, such as relaxation, creativity and romance. Or perhaps what owning a dog may give you, such as love, friendship, time for communing with nature on long walks with a furry companion… This is especially important in the reimprinting step, as it's the emotional vibration you transmit that is vital and tunes you directly into the universe – almost like having a direct telephone line.

Meet Lesley, a successful banker who worked with Susie Shelmerdine, a Matrix Reimprinting trainer with a wealth of experience in helping people realize their dreams, and who has kindly shared many of her protocols for this chapter.

Lesley desperately wanted a £1 million bonus. She'd worked in the financial sector for 10 hard years and was still at the bottom of the ladder in comparison to her male colleagues. Although £1 million bonus is bigger than most of us can ever dream of, it's all a matter of perspective and the worlds we choose to live in. Lesley's biggest block about her job was the 'unfairness' of it all – that she was doing her best to fit into this high-powered world without any of the flexibility that she needed as a mother.

As Susie and Lesley explored this belief of 'unfairness' in her life, visiting several ECHOs and collapsing the belief that life was unfair, they also spent time understanding what that bonus would actually mean for Lesley. After soul-searching, she came to the decision that once she'd got her 'golden nugget' she'd quit her job and move her entire family across the country so that she could support them financially and have the time and space to 'do motherhood properly'.

That is exactly what she did on the day she opened up the envelope containing a cheque for £1 million. It wasn't the money she wanted, but the security it would provide for her and her children. It had been a 10-year dream, and with a handful of Matrix Reimprinting sessions, she was able to achieve it in a matter of months. Perhaps more importantly, she realized that she had had the 'unfairness' belief running in her subconscious mind and that ultimately it had been her own choice to stay in that job and experience the daily unfairness of it all.

After the Matrix Reimprinting sessions, Lesley was able to see her job, her life and her beliefs in a different light and to make an empowering decision to create a new way forwards.

With Matrix Reimprinting, not only can we help clients plant healthy seeds in their inner fields, but we can also help them get congruent with their (often very private) goals, so that their vibration matches what they're transmitting to the universe.

Key Questions to Highlight Beliefs and Goal-Blockers

The truth is that most of us have limiting beliefs about creating a life that is rich and enjoyable. How can we have time *and* money? Aren't rich people evil? Do we deserve to live a life of abundance – isn't that for other people?

Now you've figured out why you want your Golden Goal, it's time to have a dig around your subconscious. Discover how you feel about that shiny goal by answering the following questions:

1. What has been holding me back from doing this?
2. Why is it important for me to be focusing on this now?
3. What are the positives to having this in my life?
4. What are the negatives to having this? What's worrying me about this goal?

The answers that you uncover will highlight where your blocks are regarding your Golden Goal. Tune in to the energy of how that feels and follow it to an ECHO.

Working with ECHOs, Goals and the Classic Technique

Once you've uncovered an ECHO, use the Classic Technique and move through the ECHO stream so that you can transform any beliefs into a new supportive platform for your life. You can also work specifically with a goal through your communication with the ECHO, using the questions above, which will help the session remain focused on the goal.

Working with ECHOs

1. Once you're in the memory and the ECHO is in a place of workability, tell the ECHO what has brought you to this particular memory, e.g. 'I am you from the future and I have found you because I am wanting [insert goal] in my life.'

2. It's likely that the ECHO will have some beliefs and energy about that goal, so tap on them to release any negative energy. When this is resolved, show the ECHO a picture or talk them through what the goal is. How does the ECHO feel about it? Does it bring up any beliefs or emotion for them? How comfortable do they feel about achieving it? Ask them if they have any advice for you.

3. Clear any fears or worries about the goal, and if you've found a limiting belief, then work on that too!

4. Use the ECHO stream technique to find other ECHOs who may feel uneasy about this goal and go back to the original core belief/memory.

5. Only once the original ECHO is fully congruent and happy/excited about achieving this goal, move to the reimprinting process. (You may want to use Positive Belief Imprinting at this point.)

◆◆◆◆◆

Positive Belief Imprinting

When combining our work with goals and connecting with the future self in Positive Belief Imprinting, working in the Matrix is a rather magical experience. Looking at our future self achieving a goal is a fantastic way to boost our success in our current reality. As we've said, it's the feeling that achieving this goal will give us that's truly important on a vibrational and cellular level.

1. Select an Issue with a Negative Field concerning One of Your Goals

Use one of the recall techniques to access specific memories and work through the Classic Technique so that you finish on the reimprinting process (*as above*).

2. Go to the Future Self

Take the ECHO to a future self where the goal has been achieved and there is a picture of success. The future self should feel completely safe and connected. How does it feel looking at that future picture? Where are you geographically? Who else is there? What can you hear? What can you smell? What's the weather like?

3. Associating with the Future ECHO

Step into the future self and feel all the energy that they feel when achieving the goal. Wash this feeling of success through every cell in the body.

4. Reimprinting Process

Step out of the ECHO and look back at the picture; make it bigger and brighter, and follow the reimprinting process where you bring in the future picture of the ECHO and send it out from your heart into the universe.

5. The 21-Day Process

You will need to reimprint the picture for 21 days.

If you are working with a client, ask them to make a note of the picture and give them these instructions to take home with them:

✧ Spend three to five minutes in the morning shortly after waking and in the evening before going to sleep reimprinting your new picture.

✧ To help the recollection of the new picture it may be useful to have a look at the note from the session about its final scene.

✧ Close your eyes and reconnect to the new picture with all your senses.

✧ Follow the reimprinting process as above so that the new picture and vibration are sent to all your cells.

6. Picture Change

If the future picture starts to feel 'uneasy', use the ECHO to go back to previous memories and clear any remaining aspects until the future picture feels positive again.

◆◆◆◆◆

The following exercises are taken from Susie Shelmerdine's empowering online programmes *Realize Your Dreams using EFT* and *Magical Relationship with Money*, which have helped hundreds of people move forwards with their dreams and transform their relationship with money.

Comfort Zones

Another way to discover goal-blocking beliefs is through exploring comfort zones. A comfort zone is a place where we feel safe or at ease, basically without stress. Stepping out of these comfort zones can mean learning new skills and raising our awareness, which can be pretty scary. We aim to build an energetic bridge between the comfort and discomfort zone, so that it becomes more comfortable to move between the two.

Ask (either yourself or a client):

✧ 'What does your comfort zone look like?' Gain as much verbal description of this 'picture' as possible.

✧ 'What does your discomfort zone look like?' Gain as much description of this 'picture' as possible.

✧ 'When you think about the goal that you've identified, does that feel as though you're in your comfort or discomfort zone?'

If the goal is in the discomfort zone, describe how that goal feels being in the discomfort zone. Give it a shape, scene or identity. Does this scene remind you of a time in your life? What do the shapes represent to you?

As soon as there's identifiable energy, you can tune in and follow it to a memory, then use the Classic Technique to reimprint.

◆◆◆◆◆

Using comfort zones is a great way to tune in to the subconscious mind and gain a representation of how you truly feel about the goal and its achievability.

Money, Money, Money

We couldn't write a chapter on goal-setting without mentioning money. Money is one of the strongest energies on Earth. All of our belief systems flow into it and we can clearly see how they reflect back at us. Unsurprisingly, it is one of the areas that people want guidance on, and it's also an area in which we can have great fun.

Try out two questions:

1. 'If money had an identity, what would it be?'

> *Meet Daniel, who saw money as an aggressive wolf who was struggling to be free. Using Matrix Reimprinting the wolf transformed into a dog. Daniel's homework between sessions was to visualize the dog and play with it every night.*
>
> *The following week he reported that it was now a puppy and whenever he thought about money, he just saw a playful puppy. After doing this work, he'd finally been able to sign a deal that he'd been working on for over two years (and was worth a lot of money to him) and he remarked, 'The block for me was in the contract. I didn't know if I could be free with it.'*

Putting an identity on money can mean we can learn what energy we've attached to it. Once we have an identity, we can go in and use Matrix Reimprinting, treat that identity as an ECHO and follow the seven steps.

2. 'If money were your lover, would you still be having sex?'

A real ice-breaker, this one, and great to use in a tapping group, as it always raises a smile. Is your money cheating on you with the bills or is it off having sex with rich people on a desert island? Does your money always have a headache? Do you want to be intimate with it?

This question opens the door to finding out what your beliefs are about money; from there you can easily tune in to the energy and resolve the surfacing memories using Matrix Reimprinting.

This is one of Caryl Westmore's case studies from *Goal Success*, revealing how she used Matrix Reimprinting to help Maryann, a frustrated writer and photographer, clear the blocks to her creative dreams:

> *Maryann was passionate about writing and photography, yet felt unable to achieve her goals of writing a book and holding a photography exhibition.*

After some initial tapping, Maryann couldn't immediately access a specific memory so they tuned in to the energy and asked her to describe that energy and how it made her feel. She responded with words like 'frustration', 'anger', 'sadness'. She checked her body to find where she was storing those feelings and described their colour as 'musty grey'.

Within minutes Maryann had traced the memory to an ECHO aged 12 years when her English teacher publicly humiliated her in front of the class for an essay she'd written. It had been a creative writing exercise.

Maryann found her ECHO outside the classroom, introduced herself and told her she had come from the future to help and support her in any way she could. By pre-warning the ECHO, the edge was taken off the shock. They froze the teacher and the class and took the ECHO out of the situation to a place where she felt safe and happy to dialogue with Maryann. They discussed what other support she wanted to call in and she mentioned her guardian angel and a wise aunt who had always encouraged her to write and paint. Maryann tapped on the ECHO in the scene, saying, 'Even though you've had a shock, you're still a beautiful little girl and you're safe.'

She continued to tap, bringing down the intensity of the shock for the ECHO by saying, 'All this shock… feeling humiliated… you thought you'd done a good job…' etc.

Once the shock was reduced, the little ECHO could hear what those who loved her had to say. She showed her aunt the essay and was assured it was a genuinely brilliant and imaginative piece of work.

The belief the little ECHO had was that she needed to please everyone. Maryann assured her that she could release that need and that most creative writers and artists learned to produce their art regardless – some people would love it, some would not, and that was all part of life.

They created a scene with lots of people, both adults and children, listening spellbound to someone reading the essay, and when it was finished, they all clapped and cheered.

Caryl and Maryann went up the ECHO stream and continued to work on some past-life events and thoroughly checked each memory for any remaining trauma before they moved to the future-self work.

Maryann asked her future self to give her some tips and wisdom on how she could be the successful writer and photographer she had become. 'How did you get to be so successful and write so many books and become acknowledged as a landscape photographer?'

Her future self dialogued with her for several minutes while Caryl held the space silently. As Maryann ended the dialogue with her future self, she described how she had been shown the way to cut emotional-energy cords between herself and close family members who were holding her back. Caryl then encouraged her to step into her future self and become her: 'Feel the feelings – joyous, successful, and creative. Revel in the feeling of recognition and happiness. Grateful for a fulfilling creative life.'

Magically, Maryann came out of her session released, relieved and inspired to start work on the several books and photography exhibitions that her future self had assured her she already had in her, waiting to be created.

Achieving our heartfelt goals and living our purpose is a possibility for all of us. It can mean not only enjoying a happier, healthier life but also becoming an inspiration for other people, empowering them to enjoy their own lives on a larger scale!

Becoming congruent with our goals is key to achieving them. How do we become congruent? We find the beliefs behind our goal-stoppers – what's holding us back from success.

What's the most creative and often the quickest way to transform them? Yep, with Matrix Reimprinting.

Chapter 16
CREATING A LIFE BEYOND BELIEF

'There are no mistakes. The events we bring upon ourselves,
no matter how unpleasant, are necessary in order to learn
what we need to learn; whatever steps we take, they're
necessary to reach the places we've chosen to go.'

RICHARD BACH

Thank you for reading this book and using Matrix Reimprinting to heal your wounds, improve your wellbeing and transform your beliefs. Why are we thanking you? Because by changing your beliefs, your personal field and your vibration, you're changing our lives too.

It's quite simple: when one person changes, the world changes. When we change our energy field, it has an effect on everyone who comes into contact with us. And we all know the difference between being in the energy field of someone who makes us feel positive and someone who makes us feel negative and drains us of our power.

Furthermore, when we move from fear to love, we not only have an impact on those with whom we come into contact, but we also weaken that huge morphic field of fear that, as humans, we all tune in to from the moment of conception.

We often mistakenly believe that we need fear in order to survive, to motivate ourselves, to stop ourselves from walking in front of a bus or into a lion's den. But we say this: we don't need fear to be intelligent.

And it's not about trying to delete fear or superimpose it, but about understanding what it's about and transforming it so that we can accept ourselves for the perfect souls that we are.

The Connection

When we do this work, we experience the connectedness of the human race and how we affect each other. The one sentence that Matrix Reimprinting practitioners hear repeatedly is: 'You'll never guess what happened after that session.'

When a young man called Michael worked with Ted Wilmont, he told him that he'd tried many different modalities to clear the problems he faced regarding intimacy with the opposite sex. Through their work together he was able to face a huge trauma in his childhood, 'a dark secret that he hadn't ever been able to tell anyone', but the process of Matrix Reimprinting make him feel safe enough.

Throughout their work together they visited his teenage ECHO, who was being teased about a photo of himself. Michael tapped on his ECHO and released the energy of feeling uncomfortable. Then he remarked that something strange had happened: 'A girl I know from school has just come into the picture and taken my ECHO's arm and walked off with him. They look happy, but it's strange – I never dated this girl at school.'

Another ECHO was in a band and making up song lyrics but being teased about his suggestions by his friends. Again Ted and Michael tapped and released the energy of feeling stupid, uncool and inadequate. Then the same girl appeared and took away the ECHO, who, incidentally, was very happy to go with her.

The next day Michael rang Ted and said, 'You'll never believe what's happened. That girl, whom I haven't been in contact with for over 11 years, found me on the internet and e-mailed me, saying, "You've been on my mind all week and I wanted to track you down and say hi."'

This is just one of hundreds of synchronicities where the work we've done in the Matrix has had an effect on our current reality. These have ranged from mothers saying 'I love you' to their children for the first time and fathers hugging their sons to book deals being signed and old friends – and old enemies – suddenly reappearing. When we work in the Matrix, it has a ripple effect similar to chaos theory, which postulates that something as small as the flap of a butterfly's wings can cause a typhoon halfway around the world.

You, our dear Matrixers, are the wind beneath that butterfly's wings, and your work helps us transform the world and show the world that we are all one.

The One Belief

We all have hundreds of beliefs, good, bad and indifferent. Beliefs that surge like rivers into our life, crashing against the rocks of our existence; and beliefs that are just tiny trickles we barely notice. Beliefs form the intricate framework for our relationships, for our parenting; they underpin our diseases and are present when we are faced with our own mortality in the process of grief.

We've seen how beliefs such as 'I have to be perfect' or 'The world is a dangerous place' soon become generalized if we don't deal with them. We'll all have one core belief that's shaping our world, and if we don't shine a light on it, it may turn all the lights out. When we're submerged in that core belief, we lose sight of who we really are: spiritual beings who are here to learn, evolve and love.

When we reduce the intensity of our core beliefs, life becomes lighter, easier and much more fun. In this lighter place, we give ourselves time to work on our goals, our body and our creative projects. We love ourselves enough to create a happy life.

Beliefs and Human Needs

We want to leave you with two tools to enhance your life: the belief brainstorm and the human needs inventory.

✧ Turn back to page 18 and reread the list of beliefs. Do any resonate with you more than others? Is it time to brainstorm all the events in your life when these beliefs were present?

✧ Make a commitment to yourself to discover those limiting beliefs and transform them into a supportive platform for the rest of your life.

✧ In conjunction with that, turn to page 139, to the human needs inventory. Where are you scoring low? Do you need some more goals or a sense of purpose in your life? What about the mind–body connection? Are you getting enough sleep or connection with others?

By combining our understanding of the belief system along with the human needs inventory, we're giving ourselves and our clients the best chance of thriving. You also have in your hands a resource to help you fulfil those needs whenever you need extra support.

A New World

Together we have created a world of distrust and fear. Why can't we change it? We all know that the old ways aren't working. Even writing about this work has brought up fear for us. We're sticking our heads above the parapet and who are we to declare we know a way to develop the human race? But in the words of Marianne Williamson, 'Who are we not to?'

We're living in the dawn of a new time, where the old paradigms are shifting. Newtonian science is being challenged by new discoveries showing us that our energy fields are connected, that we're responsible for changing our neural pathways and that our emotions are the indicators of our health.

We can all contribute to building a new field of love and trust by understanding and releasing the traumas that we've experienced. Our deepest fears are like dragons guarding our deepest treasures: these traumas are the window to our soul.

So, step into the Matrix, connect with your ECHOs and transform the limiting beliefs that are stored there. Move to a place where you do feel loved, good enough, worthy, safe and free. In the Matrix, that future is already a possibility. Go. Make it your reality.

Appendix

THE EVIDENCE BEHIND THE MATRIX MAGIC

Dr Elizabeth Boath and Professor Antony Stewart

In this era of evidence-based practice, Matrix Reimprinting, along with other Energy Psychology methods, is under ever-increasing pressure to demonstrate itself as an 'evidence-based' intervention. This demand comes in part from Matrix Reimprinting practitioners, who are keen to demonstrate the efficiency and effectiveness of their novel intervention. However, healthcare is increasingly being shaped by, for example, NHS commissioners in the UK and insurance coverage, which dictate what clients can and cannot be offered.

While single-case studies are in themselves valuable and many psychological interventions are rooted in case studies, it is essential that good-quality research in this field continues to evolve if Matrix Reimprinting is to be accepted into the mainstream. There are a growing number of Matrix Reimprinting practitioners (over 2,500 worldwide) and anecdotal evidence from a plethora of case studies demonstrating the effectiveness of Matrix Reimprinting for a wide range of issues, including: trauma, fibromyalgia, allergies, phobias, pain management, depression, anxiety and stress reduction (Dawson & Allenby, 2010).

Matrix Reimprinting is a new and evolving technique and, like all new therapies, is at the very beginning of its research journey. Research in this field is being led by Associate Professor Dr Elizabeth Boath (LB) and Professor Antony Stewart (TS) from Staffordshire University in the UK. This is the first study of its kind on Matrix Reimprinting, which the literature search of nursing, medical and psychological electronic databases using the key terms 'Matrix Reimprinting' reflects. This study is in collaboration with Sandwell Primary Care Trust and Matrix Reimprinting creator Karl Dawson (Stewart et al., 2013).

This published study is a service evaluation of an EFT/Matrix Reimprinting service in the UK, within the National Health Service (NHS). Clients presented with a range of serious disorders including anxiety and depression, trauma, sexual abuse, grief and anger.

The clients were assessed before and after Matrix Reimprinting using a number of valid (able to accurately measure what they are supposed to) and reliable scales and outcome measures. The outcome measures were CORE10, a measure of psychological distress (CORE IMS 2013), the Hospital Anxiety and Depression Scale (HADS; Zigmond and Snaith, 1983), the Rosenberg Self-Esteem Scale (Rosenberg, 1989) and the Warwick–Edinburgh Mental Wellbeing Scale (WEMWBS, 2013).

Each client was given a 10–15 minute introduction to EFT initially, and then Matrix Reimprinting was incorporated during the course of therapy. Clients receiving Matrix Reimprinting were guided through the process by TS. Initial appointments were of up to 90 minutes' duration, with each subsequent appointment lasting up to 60 minutes.

The results revealed that overall, the participants' scores on the outcome measures improved. These improvements were not only statistically significant (and therefore highly unlikely to be due to chance alone), but overall were also clinically significant (the clients met criteria as clinical 'cases' at the start, but were categorized as 'normal' at the end) following Matrix Reimprinting.

Overall, the improvements were marked. For CORE10, there was a 52% improvement in scores. Self-esteem scores improved by 46%, and anxiety reduced by 35%. The results revealed that an average of eight treatment sessions was required to treat these clients, suggesting that Matrix Reimprinting may be a very efficient and cost-effective treatment.

For a simple outline of this paper please go to: www.tinyurl.com/p6nx7z3

The second Matrix Reimprinting paper is currently being written by Dr Elizabeth Boath, Professor Anthony Stewart and Caroline Rolling, a highly experienced Matrix Reimprinting practitioner and trainer, with particular expertise in Post-Traumatic Stress Disorder. This documents the findings of a pilot study that was carried out to establish the effectiveness of Matrix Reimprinting in treating post-traumatic stress symptoms in civilian survivors of war. Over 90% of the casualties of war are civilians and thousands experienced highly traumatic events during the 1992–1995 war in Bosnia-Herzegovina. The resulting social and political upheaval meant that remarkably few mental health services were available and almost two decades after the war has ended long-term emotional issues continue.

The Healing Hands Network is a charitable organization which aims to help survivors of the war in Bosnia-Herzegovina by providing 'hands-on' therapy to people living with the mental, physical and emotional effects of the war. Matrix Reimprinting allows clients to access and transform traumatic memories and this pilot study aimed to address whether Matrix Reimprinting would be an effective and acceptable intervention in civilian survivors of war (Dawson & Allenby, 2010).

The survivors of trauma were asked to complete a modified version of a scale specifically designed to assess post-traumatic stress disorder in civilians, called the PTSD Checklist Civilian (PCL), before receiving Matrix Reimprinting and immediately after their final session at two weeks. The results showed a significant reduction in PCL scores, suggesting that Matrix Reimprinting was highly effective in treating their symptoms.

The survivors were also interviewed at the end of the study to assess their perceptions of Matrix Reimprinting. The following quotes revealed the hugely positive impact that Matrix Reimprinting had on their mental, physical and emotional lives. We let their voices speak for themselves.

> *'In the past I thought that I would never be able to overcome the traumas that I had experienced, but now I feel as though a heavy burden has been raised from my shoulders. At the beginning, I felt a huge burden on my shoulders, and my mind was filled with grey thoughts, but after only one session my mind cleared, the greyness disappeared and I felt stronger…The sessions gave me enough strength to move on with my life.' (Mira)*

> *'I feel that I've achieved so much, both physically and psychologically. I am more cheerful, calmer and happier. During the treatment I have had a nice feeling of calmness and positive emotions… My family members have noticed that I am much happier, more cheerful and definitely in a better mood.' (Amina)*

> *'These treatments are very good and I know that they will give me the strength to move on with my life.' (Harun)*

> *'I think this kind of therapy is very useful especially when it comes to psychological health – not just my own, but all the people who live in Bosnia as well.' (Hana)*

Like EFT, which over the past decade has spawned a plethora of books, research articles and publications, it is envisaged that the research into Matrix Reimprinting will continue to grow. Indeed, if Matrix Reimprinting is to throw off the cloak of 'pseudoscience' and emerge into the realm of evidence-based practice, then the need for further good-quality research is critical.

Acknowledgements

We would like to thank all of the research participants who allowed us to use their scores and quotes, and the translators. We also thank Fiona Smith for her valuable contribution in treating civilian survivors of war in Bosnia.

Useful Web Links and Resources

For more details of Matrix Reimprinting and EFT research you can look on the AAMET, ACEP and EFT Universe research web pages:

Association for the Advancement of Meridian Energy Techniques (AAMET): www.aamet.org

Association for Comprehensive Energy Psychology (ACEP): www.energypsych.org

EFT Universe Research:
www.eftuniverse.com/research-and-studies/research

About the Authors

Dr Elizabeth Boath and Prof. Antony Stewart are both academics at Staffordshire University in the UK. They are also both EFT and Matrix Reimprinting practitioners, and are leading the field in EFT and Matrix Reimprinting research in the UK.

Dr Elizabeth Boath: e.boath@staffs.ac.uk

Professor Antony Stewart: antony.stewart@staffs.ac.uk and www.eft-therapy.org

REFERENCES

Chapter 1: The Power of Belief

1. Keogh, D., and Harris, L.L. (2009), 'The placebo effect', www.nhne-pulse.org/video-the-placebo-effect (accessed 20 January 2014)

2. UK National Health Service, 'The placebo effect', www.nhs.uk/Livewell/complementary-alternative-medicine/Pages/placebo-effect.aspx (accessed 9 June 2013)

3. Montgomery, G., and Kirsch, Irving (1996), 'Mechanisms of placebo pain reduction: an empirical investigation', *Psychological Science*, Vol. 7, No. 3, pp.174–6

4. Howick, J., Bishop, F.L., Heneghan, C., Wolstenholme, J., Stevens, S., *et al.* (2013), 'Placebo use in the United Kingdom: results from a national survey of primary care practitioners', www.tinyurl.com/l8nh2w3 (accessed 10 January 2014)

5. Cited in Brogan, Kelly, MD (2013), 'A psychiatrist's perspective on using drugs', http://articles.mercola.com/sites/articles/archive/2014/01/16/dr-brogan-on-depression.aspx (accessed 20 January 2014)

6. Hamilton, David (2008), *How Your Mind Can Heal Your Body*, Hay House

7. Lipton, Bruce (2005), *The Biology of Belief*, Mountain of Love

8. Holzel, B., Carmody, J., Vangel, M., Congleton, C., Yerramsetti, S., Gard, T., Lazar, S. (2011), 'Mindfulness practice leads to increases in regional brain gray matter density', *Psychiatry Research: Neuroimaging*, Vol. 191, pp.36–43

9. Scaer, Dr Robert (2001), *The Body Bears the Burden: Trauma, Dissociation and Disease*, Haworth Medical Press, second edition, 2007, p.2

Chapter 2: The Energetic Nature of Our Universe

1. Sheldrake, Rupert (2013), Extract from speech 'The Science Delusion', Matrix Reimprinting Convention

2. Hicks, Esther and Jerry (2005), *Ask and it is Given: Learning to Manifest the Law of Attraction*, Hay House, p.114

3. Ibid., p.23

4. The Co- Intelligence Institute, 'More on morphogenetic fields', www.co-intelligence.org/P-moreonmorphgnicflds.html (accessed 10 January 2014)

5. Braden, Gregg (2007), *The Divine Matrix: Bridging Time, Space, Miracles and Beliefs*, Hay House, p.25

6. Fraser, Peter (2010), Extract from *The Living Matrix* DVD

7. Sherman, R.A., Sherman, C.J., and Parker, L. (1984), 'Chronic phantom and stump pain among American veterans: results of a survey', *Pain*, Vol. 18, pp.83–95

8. Sheldrake, Rupert (1988), *The Presence of the Past: Morphic Resonance and the Fields of Nature*, Collins; reissued Inner Traditions, Bear and Company, 2000, p.162

9. Ibid., p.167

10. Lipton, Bruce (2006), Amended extract from *As Above, So Below: An Introduction to Fractal Evolution* DVD

Chapter 4: From Emotional Freedom Technique to Matrix Reimprinting

1. Hui, K.K., *et al.* (2000), 'Acupuncture modulates the limbic system and subcortical gray structures of the human brain: evidence from fMRI studies in normal subjects', *Human Brain Mapping*, Vol. 9, no. 1, pp.13–25; Fang, J., *et al.* (2009), 'The salient characteristics of the central effects of acupuncture needling: limbic-paralimbic-neocortical network modulation', *Human Brain Mapping*, Vol. 30, no. 4, pp.1,196–206

2. Feinstein, D. (2008), 'Energy Psychology: a review of the preliminary evidence', *Psychotherapy: Theory, Research, Practice, Training*, Vol. 45, No. 2, pp.199–213

Chapter 5: The Four Principles of Matrix Reimprinting

1. Childre, Doc and Martin, Howard (1999), *The HeartMath Solution*, HarperCollins, p.24

2. McCraty *et al.* (1999), 'The role of physiological coherence in the detection and measurement of cardiac energy exchange between people', *Proceedings of the Tenth International Montreux Congress on Stress*, Montreux, Switzerland, cited in www.heartmath.org/about-us/our-focus/science-research.html (accessed 21 September 2013)

3. www.heartmath.org (accessed 2 May 2014)

Chapter 6: The Classic Matrix Reimprinting Technique

1. To find out more about the SUE scale, please see Silvia Hartmann's *Positive EFT* (2013), which is available from DragonRising Publishing (www.dragonrising.com/store/positive_eft) or all good bookshops.

Chapter 8: Conscious Parenting

1. Lipton, Bruce (2005), *The Biology of Belief*, Mountain of Love; Hay House edition, 2011, p.142

2. Verny, Thomas, and Weintraub, Pamela (2003), *Pre-Parenting: Nurturing Your Child from Conception*, Simon and Schuster

3. Bea, R.H. Van den Bergh *et al.* (2005), 'Antenatal maternal anxiety and stress and the neurobehavioral development of the fetus and

child: links and possible mechanisms. A review', *Neuroscience and Biobehavioral Reviews*, Vol. 29, issue 2, pp.237–58

4. Hay, Louise (1984), *You Can Heal Your Life*, Hay House, p.4

5. Markham, Dr Laura (2012), *Peaceful Parents, Happy Kids*, Penguin Books, p.8

6. Lipton, Bruce (2005), *The Biology of Belief*, Mountain of Love

7. Tolle, Eckhart (2011), www.eckharttolle.com/newsletter/june-2011 (accessed November 2013)

8. Mendizza, Michael and Chilton Pearce, Joseph (2001), *Magical Parent, Magical Child: The Art of Joyful Parenting*, North Atlantic Books

9. Cited in Perrow, Susan (2011), *Healing Stories for Challenging Behaviour*, Hawthorn Press, p.2

Chapter 9: Moving through Stress, Anxiety and Depression

1. World Health Organization, *The Global Burden of Disease: 2004 Update*, pp.43–4

2. www.humangivenscollege.com

3. The Human Givens Institute: www.hgi.org.uk (accessed 5 May 2014)

Chapter 10: Managing Pain in the Matrix

1. UK National Health Service, 'Complex Regional Pain Syndrome', www.nhs.uk/conditions/Complex-regional-pain-syndrome/Pages/Introduction.aspx (accessed 10 November 2013))

2. Sherman, R.A., Sherman, C.J., and Parker, L. (1984), 'Chronic phantom and stump pain among American veterans: results of a survey', *Pain*, Vol. 18, pp.83–95

3. Thorpe, Sam (2013), *Meta Messages from Your Body*, The Successful Author, p.102

4. Hay, Louise (1984), *You Can Heal Your Life*, Hay House, p.182

Chapter 11: Recovering from Abuse

1. Scaer, Dr Robert (2001), *The Body Bears the Burden: Trauma,*

Dissociation and Disease, Haworth Medical Press, second edition, 2007, p.2

2. Garvin, M.C., Tarullo, A.R., Van Ryzin, M., Gunnar, M.R. (2012), 'Post-adoption parenting and socioemotional development in post-institutionalized children', *Development and Psychopathology*, Vol. 24, pp.35–48

3. McElvaney, Jeanne (2013), *Healing Insights: Effects of Abuse for Adults Abused as Children*, CreateSpace Independent Publishing Platform

Chapter 13: Clearing Phobias and Allergies

1. World Health Organization (2002), *Report on Prevention of Allergy and Allergic Asthma*, www.tinyurl.com/oudfghn (accessed 10 January 2014)

2. Mills, E.N., Mackie, A. R., Burny, P., Beyer, K., Frewer, L. *et al.* (2007), 'The prevalence, cost and basis of food allergy across Europe', *Allergy*, Vol. 62, pp.717–22

3. World Health Organization, *White Book on Allergy 2011–2012*, Executive Summary

Chapter 14: Loving Your Body Image

1. Ortner, Nick (2013), *The Tapping Solution*, Hay House, p.110

Appendix: The Evidence Behind the Matrix Magic

1. Dawson, K. & Allenby, S. (2010). *Matrix Reimprinting using EFT*. London: Hay House.

2. CORE IMS Ltd. Online at www.coreims.co.uk/index.html (accessed 12/10/2013).

3. Rosenberg, M. (1989). *Society and the Adolescent Self-Image*. Revised edition. Middletown, CT: Wesleyan University Press.

4. Stewart, A., Boath, E., Carryer, A., Walton, I., Hill, L. & Dawson, K. (2013). Can Matrix Reimprinting Be Effective in the Treatment of Emotional Conditions in a Public Health Setting? Results of a UK Pilot Study. *Energy Psychology Journal*, DOI: 0.9769. EPJ.2013.5.1.AS.EB.AC.IW.LH.DP.KD.

5. Warwick–Edinburgh Mental Wellbeing Scale (WEMWBS) Online at: www.healthscotland.com/documents/1467.aspx (accessed 12/10/2013).

6. Zigmond A.S. & Snaith R.P. (1983). The hospital anxiety and depression scale. *ActaPsychiatrica Scandinavica* 67(6): 361–370.

7. Boath, E., Stewart, T. and Rolling C. (2014). The Impact of EFT and Matrix Reimprinting on the Civilian Survivors of War in Bosnia: A Pilot Study. Curr. Res. Psychol., 5: 64–72. www.thescipub.com/abstract/10.3844/crpsp.2014.64.72

RESOURCES FOR PRACTITIONERS

We hope you've enjoyed this initial delve into the Matrix to transform your beliefs. Whilst we encourage even the novice to try Matrix Reimprinting, you'll have the most success if you take a practitioner course. These are held around the world. You can find details of one near you by visiting www.matrixreimprinting.com. Details of the practitioner process are as follows:

Step 1: Have a Good Knowledge of EFT

You will either have to attend a three-day EFT Practitioner Course or Matrix Reimprinting Introductory Course so that you are trained to Level 2 or have extensive previous EFT experience.

If you are qualified or experienced in using EFT, you do not need to attend an introductory course and you can go straight to Step 2 and attend the two-day Matrix Reimprinting Practitioner Training.

We consider you qualified and experienced in EFT if you are EFT Level 2 and above.

Alternatively, if you have extensively studied Gary Craig's DVD Library or the Gold Standard EFT Tutorial, and put your learning into practice, you can also go straight to Step 2.

Step 2: Attend a Two-Day Matrix Reimprinting Practitioner Training

Step 3: Register

Having attended the two-day training, practitioner trainees need to register on the Matrix Reimprinting website so that they can access approximately 15 hours of required viewing.

Step 4: Take the Exam

Having watched the videos, trainees have an online Matrix Reimprinting exam to complete in order to achieve practitioner status. Having successfully completed this exam (pass 40/50), they will be e-mailed a Matrix Reimprinting Practitioner certificate.

CONTRIBUTORS

This book has been a collaborative effort with many Matrix Reimprinting trainers and practitioners across the world and it belongs to them as much as it does to Karl and Kate. If you've an interest in a specific area or have resonated with the ideas or exercises in a certain chapter, then please go to their website, as they'll have much more information to share with you.

Conscious Parenting

Erika Brodnock
www.karismakidz.co.uk

Erika Brodnock is one of the UK's leading experts on the subject of raising happy, successful children. Erika founded the Karisma Kidz brand to help children identify and manage their emotions and teach them to 'Unleash the Superhero Within!'

Sharon King
www.magicalnewbeginnings.com

Sharon King is the creator of the Matrix Birth Reimprinting protocol, which helps you transform your experience of birth. She is also the author of an exciting new book which introduces a new paradigm in conscious birthing.

Move through Stress, Anxiety and Depression

Jemima Eames

www.jemimaeames.com

Jemima Eames specializes in identifying and transforming the underlying beliefs that trigger overwhelming emotions and subsequent behaviour patterns of stress and anxiety.

Jill Wootton

www.within-sight.com

Jill has helped thousands of people with depression and anxiety back to wellness. Using a fusion of traditional and Energy Psychology, she teaches, coaches and mentors individuals and groups to create the life and business they love.

Sally-Ann Soulsby

www.innerwisdom.co.uk

Transforming Lives, Finding Wholeness: Sally-Ann Soulsby is a BACP-accredited therapist and trainer pioneering the integration of mainstream therapies and Energy Psychology. She lives and loves what she teaches!

Managing Pain in the Matrix

Carey Mann

www.careymann.com

Carey Mann is a pain-relief coach who specializes in working with all types of chronic pain and has a special interest in RSD/CRPS and chronic injury.

Rob van Overbruggen PhD

www.helpforhealth.com

Rob is an international speaker, author and mentor on emotions and health. He helps people to gain emotional and physical health. His book, *Healing Psyche*, about emotions and cancer, has become the authority in many mind–body clinics worldwide.

Sam Thorpe

www.intoalignment.com

Sam is a Professional Energist specializing in stress and trauma and their relationship with disease. She works as a consultant and master trainer of Meta-Health, and of EFT, EmoTrance and other energy therapy techniques.

Recovering from Abuse

Caroline Paulzen

www.efttraining.com.au

Specializing in empowering women to overcome and heal from any type of abuse with Matrix Reimprinting as a fundamental tool.

Coping with Grief and Loss

Kathy Adams

www.kathyadamshealth.co.uk

Kathy works with people with serious physical and emotional issues, bringing an integrative approach combining counselling, wellness coaching and teaching, energy psychology and homoeopathy.

Janice Thompson

www.janicethompson.co.uk

Janice Thompson is an emotional health consultant who works with modern Energy Psychology techniques, specializing in helping those who are experiencing grief or any other type of loss. To download Janice's Smartphone app 'Hearts of Grief', please go direct to her website.

Loving Your Body Image

Corah Clark

www.corah.me

Corah Clark works with clients to uncover the underlying beliefs and patterns that hold them back from expressing their authentic and truly unique selves.

Wendy Fry

www.bepositive.me.uk

Wendy Fry is an emotional health and weight-management consultant and specializes in working with women and children to maintain their emotional wellbeing. Wendy is also the author of *Find You, Find Love: Get to the Heart of Relationships using EFT*.

Achieve Our Goals

Susie Shelmerdine

www.susieshelmerdine.com

International trainer Susie Shelmerdine is a specialist in inspiring and empowering people to realize their dreams in business and in life.

Caryl Westmore

www.breakfreefast.com and www.goalsuccessyes.com

Caryl Westmore is an EFT-Matrix Reimprinting and Matrix Goals Reimprinting author, trainer and coach who works with clients who are ready to 'break free – fast – to live the life you love', specializing in goals like soul-mate love, life purpose and writing/marketing a Kindle book.

The Science behind the Matrix

Dr Elizabeth Boath

Dr Elizabeth Boath is an academic psychologist and Associate Professor in Health at Staffordshire University and specializes in health and wellbeing research.

Professor Antony Stewart

www.eft-therapy.org and www.staffs.ac.uk/staff/profiles/as23.jsp

Antony Stewart is a Matrix Reimprinting practitioner and trainer, EFT advanced practitioner and trainer and clinical hypnotherapist. As Professor in Public Health at Staffordshire University, he has published research on both Matrix Reimprinting and EFT.

Special Thanks Also Go to...

Sasha Allenby

www.sashaallenby.com

Sasha Allenby, co-author of Matrix Reimprinting Using EFT, is now coaching therapists, motivational speakers and spiritual entrepreneurs to write their self-help and transformational books. See her book *Write Your Self-Help Book in 12 Weeks: The Definitive Guide for Spiritual Entrepreneurs* or go to her website sashaallenby.com for free resources and more information.

Amy Branton

www.freehearteft.co.uk

Amy empowers you to transform limiting beliefs to ones that reflect the limitless abundance within you and helps you to live from your heart's unique wisdom and guidance.

Penny Croal

www.changeahead.biz

Penny Croal is a master Meta-Health trainer/coach as well as a Matrix Reimprinting and EFT master trainer specializing in serious disease and women's midlife, guiding clients by finding the root cause of all illness and dis-ease and empowering them to health and a natural balance of choice and vitality.

Alexa Garside

www.alexagarside.com

brightonillustrators.co.uk/portfolios/alexa_garside

Alexa Garside is an artist and illustrator from Brighton, UK. She has been drawing since she could pick up a pencil and comes from a family of animators and artists. Alexa has a history in publishing and print work and enjoys working on book covers and internal illustrations for a wide range of different genres, applying many different styles.

Vera Malbaski

www.veraeft.com

Vera is an EFT and Matrix Reimprinting trainer and travels extensively throughout Spain and Latin America, teaching in both Spanish and English.

Pia Mark

www.heartfulhealing.co.uk

Pia Mark is an EFT and Matrix Reimprinting practitioner specializing in helping people uncover and heal the deeper core issues involved in stress and anxiety, both the underlying day-to-day stress and any stress-related illness.

Caroline Rolling

www.carolinerolling.com

Forces Family Help: Caroline Rolling specializes in helping forces' and veterans' families, including children of all ages, to ride the storm and find a balance.

Ted Wilmont

ted@eft4life.co.uk

Ted is one of the most experienced EFT and Matrix Reimprinting practitioner/trainers in the world. His vision is for all of us to live consciously without fear.

ACKNOWLEDGEMENTS

We would both like to thank Sasha Allenby for her contribution to this work with the first book, *Matrix Reimprinting Using EFT*.

Silvia Hartmann and the AMT (Association for Meridian and Energy Therapies) continue to pioneer Energy Psychology techniques across the world, and it's thanks to their proliferation that we have tools such as the SUE scale and Slow EFT.

Thanks also to the team at Hay House, especially Amy Kiberd for her joyful presence and belief in our work.

Kate

First, I'd like to thank Karl. When I collected my first EFT certificate from him and was desperate to be published, he gave me a hug and whispered, 'Kate the author,' into my ear. Who knew that five years later we would co-author this book?

There are four friends who have been my cheerleaders throughout this journey. They Matrixed with me, they listened and most of all they had the absolute unwavering belief that I could write this book. Aisling O'Gorman, Ros Barber, Jemima Eames and Cat Curtis, this book is for you.

I'm blessed with a supportive, dynamic and large family and friendship circle who, while they might not be into EFT and Matrix Reimprinting, have always supported me. It's appreciated.

To my parents, Patrick and Irene, thank you for always loving me, even when it hurt, and believing that I would change. And, you know what? I did.

Thank you to my sisters, Rebecca and Jennifer, for your love and support (and to the inventors of Facetime for keeping us connected).

To my second set of parents, David and Linda Harris. I'm so lucky to have you in my life as a constant source of advice, fun and laughter.

To my magical husband, Nigel – I got lucky when I met you! Thank you for everything. I could not have done this without you. Words don't cover how grateful I am for your love and support.

Finally, to Kieran. I wrote this through your 'terrible twos' and whenever I needed a reality check, there you were, ready to jump on my back and do 'horsey' around the living room.

Karl

To my kind and loving parents, Pam and Gordon, and my sister, Caroline, who gave up a 25-year nursing career to follow her little brother on this path. Very proud of you, sis!

To Adele. My guiding star brought us back together after 10 years apart; you are an amazing woman, whose kindness, loyalty to family and friends, strength and wisdom are limitless.

To my amazing children, Daniel and Meaghan. I'm sorry I wasn't there for you as you were growing into the wonderful young adults you are today. Daniel, I admire your drive and ambition, and my caring little Princess Meaghan, I know you will change the world.

To my best friends, Ted and CJ, who have been a huge part of my family for 25 years; Donna, for helping me keep organized; Sasha, for the huge success of the first book; the Matrix gang who have been there since the beginning; Carey, Susie, Penny, Sharon and all the other Matrix trainers and practitioners who have helped Matrix evolve over the years.

And to Kate, for being brave enough to take on the huge task of writing this book. Never doubted you for a minute.

INDEX

WANT TO TRY MATRIX REIMPRINTING IN PERSON?

How about a 50% discount on your first session?

We know you've learned the basics, but perhaps it's time to work with a Matrix Reimprinting practitioner who can expertly guide you in the Matrix.

Our community is so passionate about sharing this great technique with you that practitioners have agreed that all readers of this book will receive a 50% discount for their first session.

What you need to do:

✧ Go to www.matrixreimprinting.com and search by either practitioner name or your location.

✧ Once you've found your practitioner of choice, contact them and let them know that you have a copy of *Transform Your Beliefs, Transform Your Life* and would like to use the code MATRIX50 to gain the 50% discount on your first session.

There is a thriving community of over 3,000 practitioners across the world. If there isn't one near you, Skype can work effectively for your session.

Terms & Conditions
This offer is only valid for the first session for a new client. The Matrix Reimprinting practitioner has full discretion as to whether they want to take on new clientele. Matrix Reimprinting Ltd is not responsible for the individual knowledge or skills of practitioners listed on www. matrixreimprinting.com

ABOUT THE AUTHORS

 **Karl Dawson** is the creator of Matrix Reimprinting and one of only 29 EFT Founding Masters worldwide. Karl has taught thousands of students from all over the globe how to transform their emotional health by releasing stress and trauma.

www.matrixreimprinting.com and www.karldawson.org

 **Kate Marillat** combines her expert knowledge of Matrix Reimprinting and creativity to ease people into a state of flow. Through personal sessions, online courses and workshops, you will transform your beliefs about living a creative life, eliminate procrastination and develop a deep respect for your imaginative work and emotional wellbeing.

www.katemarillat.com and www.eftbrighton.com

Made in the USA
San Bernardino, CA
02 September 2014